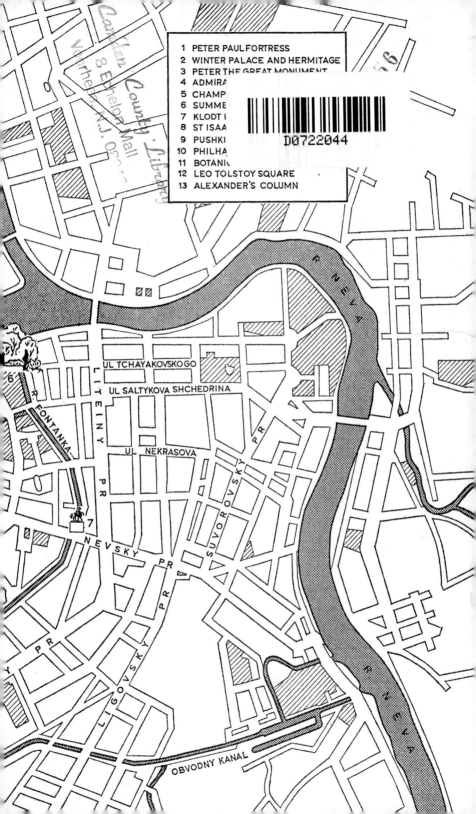

1 PETER PAUL FORTRESS
2 WINTER PALACE AND HERMITAGE
3 PETER THE GREAT MONUMENT
4 ADMIRA
5 CHAMP
6 SUMME
7 KLODT
8 ST ISAA
9 PUSHKI
10 PHILHA
11 BOTANI
12 LEO TOLSTOY SQUARE
13 ALEXANDER'S COLUMN

D0722044

UL TCHAYAKOVSKO GO

UL SALTYKOVA SHCHEDRINA

UL NEKRASOVA

R NEVA

LITEINY PR

FONTANKA

SUVOROVSKY PR

7

NEVSKY PR

PR

OBVODNY KANAL

Vera Inber, Leningrad, 1943

Leningrad Diary

Vera Inber

Translated by Serge M. Wolff
and Rachel Grieve

With an Introduction by
Edward Crankshaw

ST. MARTIN'S PRESS

AFFILIATED PUBLISHERS: Macmillan & Company, Limited.
London – also at Bombay, Calcutta, Madras and Melbourne –
The Macmillan Company of Canada, Limited, Toronto

Translator's dedication

To the people of Leningrad and the memory of my parents
in gratitude for a happy childhood

S.M.W.

Vera Inber

by Harrison Salisbury

The coming of the war changed life for everyone in Russia and for few more than for Vera Inber, the poet, and her husband, Professor Ilya Davidovich Strashun.

Vera Inber was not a Leningrader. When the Nazi attack struck Russia so unexpectedly on 22nd June, 1941, she and her husband, a prominent physician, were living comfortably in Moscow, a middle-aged, well-placed couple, grandparents, prominent Soviet citizens who had reached the point in their lives when they could look forward to comparative ease and peace.

On 27th August, 1941, the Leningrad writer Vera Ketlinskaya was hard at work in the fine old stone mansion at No. 18 Ulitsa Voinova, near the Neva embankment, which was the office of the Leningrad Writers Union. She was helping writers with wartime problems, arranging assignments for them, assisting those who wished to be evacuated from Leningrad, putting them in touch with military units—handling the multitude of chores which had suddenly come into being with the war. She looked up from her desk to see the office door open and a small graceful woman with grey hair enter. It was Vera Inber.

Vera Ketlinskaya could not have been more surprised. Why was Vera Inber in Leningrad rather than Moscow? The answer was a simple one. Vera Inber told her friend that she and her husband had come to live in Leningrad. 'I don't know for how long, but at least until spring,' she added.

Vera Ketlinskaya was astounded. The Germans on that day were thundering at the very near approaches to the city. At any moment they might break into the streets. The city was threatened with encirclement. Indeed, it might already be in a state of siege. She cleared the room and began to talk of this with Vera Inber.

The Moscow writer simply brushed all such talk aside. She

and her husband, she said, had a choice. He could be chief of a hospital far to the rear in northern Archangel or in Leningrad.

'We decided,' Vera Inber said, 'that since my daughter and grandson have been evacuated and since, as a poet, I should in time of war be in the centre of events, naturally Leningrad would be much more interesting.'

Besides, she said, she was confident that Leningrad would not be overrun. Moreover, she and her husband were not young and 'for the middle-aged to sit in the rear is somehow very shameful'.

Vera Inber did not 'sit in the rear'. She had reached Leningrad at the final moment before the city went under siege. Her train was one of the very last to press through before the Germans cut the line. The station of Mga, a peaceful out-of-the-way point just outside the city, which she describes in the entry '23rd August, 1941, Unknown Station', fell to the Nazis 24 hours after her talk with Vera Ketlinskaya. With the fall of Mga the encirclement of Leningrad was complete. The 900-day siege had begun.

I read all of the Leningrad diaries to which I could gain access in writing my *The 900 Days—The Siege of Leningrad*. I know of no other diary which gives so intimate and at the same time panoramic view of life in Leningrad from the inception of the siege to its lifting in 1944. Vera Inber saw it all and recorded it with the observation and meticulous sensitivity of a poet. Here it is—the terrible air attack and destruction of the famous Badaev warehouses which housed a major portion of Leningrad's food reserves in the Nazi bombardment of 8th September, 1941; the feeling of isolation when the telephone rang on the morning of 16th September, 1941, and the operator announced that 'the telephone is disconnected until the end of the war'; the distress at the news of the fall of Kiev; the haunting days when she and her husband and his hospital lived in apprehension while an enormous unexploded bomb which had fallen in the hospital courtyard was being extricated.

The entries of the autumn of 1941 race ahead, each week bringing news more desperate both inside Leningrad and for Russia as a whole—the fall of Orel, the fall of Odessa, the Germans closing their ring around Moscow. And in Leningrad the siege tighter and tighter, the city more and more grim. The first hints of starvation (more than a million persons ultimately were to die) when Vera Inber's friend, Marietta, reports that the guinea pigs and rabbits have vanished from her experimental laboratory. The bread ration reduced. Reduced again. Reduced again until by late November it was a slice of bread a day (125 grams). By now she is recording that people are eating their cats and dogs.

Vera Inber's chronicle is an honest one. When she loses her nerve and temper in the exhaustion of the siege days she records the incident (an old woman is searching for lost ration cards on the pavement in the blackout and appeals for help; Vera Inber snaps 'Look for yourself!' but her husband stops and finds the lost cards—had the cards not been found the woman would certainly have starved to death). Electricity goes off. The realisation sets in that Leningrad may not survive. On 1st December she records seeing the first small sled bearing a corpse, the first of tens of thousands, until the frozen corpses were piled in such mounds in the streets near the morgues, the hospitals and the cemeteries that traffic no longer could pass. Yet, even in these times, the orchestra wearing sheepskin coats, the hall lighted with candles or a few light bulbs, the Philharmonic continued to give concerts.

Yet the worst lies ahead. A bomb knocks out the water supply and sewer system of her husband's hospital. Soon the whole city is without water and sewers—all frozen. There is no transportation except a few military vehicles. Everyone must walk, feeble as they are. The electricity dwindles to nothing. The dead begin to pile up outside Erisman Hospital (her husband's) like cordwood. The bread ration rises on Christmas Day (but by now people are dying at a rate of six thousand or more a day). By the New Year the streets were filled with sleds and people trying, pitifully, to bring the corpses to assembly points. Vera Inber had come to the point at which she could not stand the smell of the pine extract with which the corpses were doused for sanitary reasons. Now, as Vera Inber recorded, 'Leningrad is living at the expense of the last remnants of its strength.'

The bitterness deepens. By 3rd January, 1942, she is writing: 'There were rejoicings on the day the bread ration was increased by 75 grams but that was a long time ago.' (It was nine days earlier!)

Ahead lay the whole winter of 1942, the most terrible time any city has endured—a winter and an ordeal which wore

Vera Inber to the very margin of survival. Day after day she writes: 'Shall we have enough strength to wait for the Blockade to lift? And how many will be alive to rejoice that they live?'

Disappointment followed disappointment. There had been a great buoying of hope at Christmas time, a feeling that delivery, that food would be getting through to the city. The ice road across Lake Ladoga had been opened, but it would be many weeks before the supplies arrived in such quantities as to begin to ameliorate suffering and, in part, this was only possible because by that time more hundreds of thousands of people had died, reducing the burden.

I think it is impossible for anyone who did not, like Vera Inber, survive that satanic winter of 1942 to catch its feeling. Even when reading her words: 'Our position is catastrophic. Just now a crowd destroyed the wooden fence of the hospital grounds and carried it away for firewood. There is no water and if the bakery stops even for a single day what happens? We have no soup, only porridge. In the morning there was coffee but there won't be any more to drink.'

Well, the bakery *did* halt. Toward the end of January *all* power ceased in Leningrad. There was no bread for several days (Vera Inber says it didn't stop; that 8,000 young Communists kept the bakery going with a bucket brigade to supply water; actually many in the city did not receive bread for several days; more tens of thousands died).

By spring Vera Inber (and almost everyone still surviving in Leningrad) was in a state of full nervous and physical exhaustion. As she writes on 31st March: 'What will happen to us? What will become of me? I don't know. I know nothing. I am distressed and very much afraid to write about it without false shame. I AM AFRAID. . . .'

Finally spring comes and she writes: 'Pale, exhausted, weak people (dystrophy, second degree) make their way here slowly, screwing up their eyes against the spring sun, wondering that they are still alive. Sometimes they sit down and rest, exposing to the sun's rays a bare arm or leg covered in scurvy scores.'

By this time it was apparent that Leningrad by some means had survived, but the toll in human life was in the vicinity of 1,200,000. Possibly more. No one was ever to know. How many were left alive is not certain either. There were probably 2,500,000 in the city when the blockade started. Now, 1st April, 1942, there were about 1,100,000. No other city in the history of the world had passed through anything comparable to this.

Nor was it yet over, as Vera Inber makes clear. For the Nazis were to try to take the city. They were to bombard it again and again and again by air and by long-range guns, particularly in the spring of 1942. Not until January, 1943, would a winter offensive make a real dent in the Nazi encirclement. With the recapture of Schlisselburg it became possible to restore tenuous land supply to Leningrad via a railroad link that passed within 500 yards of German guns. And not until 27th January, 1944, was Vera Inber able to write in her diary:

'The greatest event in the life of Leningrad—complete liberation from the Blockade. And here words fail me, a professional writer. I simply say Leningrad is free. And there isn't any more to be said.'

Vera Inber and Dr. Strashun lingered a few more weeks in Leningrad before leaving on June 12 to return to their home in Moscow. Before they left they went to see an exhibit of the Defence of Leningrad, a tribute to the heroism and suffering of the city. There they saw 'our bomb', the very one which had fallen in the hospital grounds in September, 1941; they saw all the statistics; they read again the formula for Leningrad bread (root flour, sweepings, flour from linseed cakes, cellulose), the fish glue and hides used for soup and jellies; the 125-gram ration Leningrad had lived on from 20th November, 1941 to 25th December, 1941. Then they went home and packed for Moscow. The Leningrad epic, it seemed, had come to an end. Little did they know that another fateful chapter remained to be written—the so-called 'Leningrad Affair', one of Stalin's paranoid plots directed against the leaders of Leningrad who had brought the city through its terrible travail, and also against many of the most heroic of Leningrad's citizens. Even the exhibition which Vera Inber and her husband visited would be closed and its artifacts, records, and mementos scattered into police vaults or simply destroyed so that for many in Russia it is only by reading diaries like Vera Inber's that something of the terror and the courage can be recaptured. Stalin actually tried literally to wipe out of memory the Leningrad apocalyse. But of course he did not succeed. The heroism and bravery of Leningrad and its men and women, as Vera Inber records, will live forever.

Introduction

by Edward Crankshaw

I have always felt that the only fitting memorials to those who died in the siege of Leningrad must be the personal records of individual survivors, because the reality of this terrible, all but incredible story was the sum of the endurance of countless individuals.

The sum was monstrous. The siege lasted for nine hundred days. More than three million people were trapped in Peter the Great's immense granite show-piece of a city, built on a swamp on the northern fringe of Europe. More than a million of them died, many under the merciless bombing and shelling, but most of hunger and cold. The main food depots went up in flames in the first week of the siege, on 6th September, 1941. Winter came early that year, and it turned out to be the hardest winter for a hundred years. I myself was in Russia throughout that winter, a soldier attached to the British Military Mission, and heard a great deal of what was being said and written in the West about the way the extreme cold had come to the aid of the Red Army and was punishing the Germans in front of Moscow. What was not so well appreciated was that the winter of 1941–2 came close to finishing off the Russians too. In all the cities and towns of central and northern Russia, including Moscow itself, the less strong were dying of hunger and cold. In Leningrad the strong died too. But Leningrad endured. The people lived or died on a handful of black bread a day in buildings that were tombs—dead, unlit, unheated in fifty degrees of frost. They were saved in extremity, those who survived, only by the famous ice 'road of life' across Lake Ladoga, which was somehow kept open at fearful cost and under incessant bombardment.

Before that they had saved themselves. More than a million of them, men, women and children, went out to dig trenches and fortify strong-points in the city suburbs, manned by factory and office workers. Mechanics from the Kirov works, untrained in warfare, drove off the tanks as they finished building them, still unpainted, straight into battle a mile or so down the road, to fill gaps in the ranks of a shattered army. They had to save themselves because nobody else would save them.

Everybody in the Soviet Union knew about the suffering in Leningrad, but it was not until years later that survivors were able to tell their story publicly. The whole story is perhaps too complex and overpowering ever to be told. Instead there have lately been a multitude of personal narratives. The diary of the distinguished poet, Vera Inber, who lived through the whole of the siege, has long been recognised as a classic among these. It is a day-to-day account of the struggle for survival in conditions of, to us, inconceivable hardship, illuminated by a subtle intelligence and the exact, cool eye of the artist: even when reduced by hunger and cold to the point sometimes of hallucination, sometimes of virtual inanition, she can describe (cannot help describing) in winged words the terrible beauty of aspects of universal death.

About her wonderful narrative there is nothing to be said, except that it is an honour to introduce it to the English-speaking world. In writing of her experiences she speaks for tens, for hundreds, of thousands of others. And terrible as her own condition was, for most of these others the horror was even more absolute. Dumb victims, unsupported by the inner resources and the vision which sustained the artist, they held on until they died or miraculously came through, because it was the only thing to do. Here they find their voice in the narrative of a poet who celebrates their courage while making little of her own.

None of them knew it at the time, but surrender in fact would have meant mass destruction. Hitler had issued a formal command: the people of Leningrad were to be starved and bombarded into submission. They were then to be driven out into the snowy waste to die, and the city was to be systematically destroyed, erased from the face of the earth and never rebuilt. 'After the defeat of Russia there will not be the slightest reason for the existence of this large city.' It is still there.

The Diary

The train has stopped. Two bomb craters are joined together
to form a huge cavity. A smashed tanker lies nearby, and the
surrounding earth is dark with the oil that has poured from it.
A burnt-out railway engine lies at the bottom of the embankment. There is a pre-war sign saying 'ANYONE SMOKING WILL
BE PROSECUTED'. A signal woman with a tear-stained face holds
us up with a flag which she waves listlessly. She is far gone in
pregnancy.

We stop again. Trucks come towards us loaded with
machinery and covered with birch branches. They come from
Leningrad factories that are being evacuated. One can judge the
time these trains spend on their way by the freshness of the
branches. The trucks carry fly wheels, cog wheels, lathes,
small machine parts, all kept separate, carefully greased and
wrapped in parchment. Behind come the vans that carry the
workers' families; these vans are heated by stoves, and in one
carriage there are children on hard plank beds . . . the children,
huddled together, look out of the window. There isn't a smile
amongst them.

In Moscow they told me that in the rush of the evacuation
each child had its name written on its little hand with an
indelible pencil, but that when the destination was reached
they were all given baths and the names were washed off. The
mothers had to be called from Moscow in order to sort out
the children—and one child remains unidentified. . . . Oh, my
dear Moscow! I have left it behind, but it doesn't leave me . . .
it follows me, rending my heart. I keep seeing my little grandson Mishenka; he is only six months old. He was left wearing
an open shirt and a linen cap that was too big for him on his
darling little head. He was put into a children's compartment
and he lay very still, looking at everyone with shining eyes,
gripping his tiny leg with his hand. . . . I hadn't the courage to

go back and have a last look at him . . . and so he was carried away.

Our train is moving at last, and so is the goods train. We are going to Leningrad and it is coming away . . . we are able to see it for a long time.

23 August, 1941. Unknown Station

We have stopped at dawn, and we are still here. The station is some way away, and is unknown to us. There isn't a plane in the air, and no guns are firing from the ground. . . . I would rather hell were let loose, anything would be easier to bear than this dead silence.

The carriage is fairly empty, no one talks much. In one compartment an endless card game is in progress; a general whistles thoughtfully as he declares his suit, an army engineer knocks out his pipe on the table corner, over and over again. It is a quiet sound, and it reminds me of a woodpecker tapping its tree. The pipe smoke drifts into the corridor, moves in layers, thins out and is suspended in the rays of the sun. Everything is so quiet, it seems as if the train is resting on moss.

In all this long time only two Hawk fighter planes have come over us, and a small detachment of Marines has passed by, their golden anchors flashing in the sunshine . . . there are no other signs of life.

On either side of the railway line there are craters filled with water, and smaller craters beside the telegraph poles. The Germans have, as usual, been cheese-paring—using high-explosive bombs for the railway, little bombs being good enough for the telegraph line . . . we are moving now, and we pass dead woods, all the earth scorched by explosives. In one place all the trees are torn out, and their roots point upwards . . . and there is the bark of a small birch tree—all tiny dots, stripes and spots—it makes me think of a shorthand record—here is the whole history of its life, and now this history is cut short in the middle of a sentence. Everything is split, charred, dead.

I have just learned the name of the station. It is Mga. We never knew this line before the war, as we always travelled on the Oktiabrskaya line. But now this is no longer possible because the Germans are between Bologoe and Tosno . . . and what resinous names the places have, in these parts—Mga,

Bydgoshch, Khvoinaya [meaning pine needles—translator's note].

24th August, 1941. Leningrad

The first thing we see while we are still in the station square is an appeal signed by Zhukov, Voroshilov and Popkov. The posters have been stuck on walls that are bathed in sunshine. We read: 'COMRADES, LENINGRADERS, DEAR FRIENDS . . .' This appeal appeared on the 21st August, and Ilya Davidovitch had come to Moscow to fetch me on the 13th. During that time the position of Leningrad has worsened drastically, but my husband had done the right thing in coming for me. He always said, 'If war breaks out we should be together.' And here we are—together.

26th August, 1941

Our flat is in the Pesochnaya, on the fifth floor. The rooms are high, light and half empty. Nothing but bookcases, and plates on the wall in great profusion. They are very fine old plates, and the roses bloom forever on the porcelain of the Empresses Elisabeth and Catherine the Great. The blue and gold borders of the dishes are as fresh as the day they were painted in the reign of Nicholas I . . . these are fragile things, what on earth can we do with them now?

Our bedroom windows and the balcony face the Botanical Gardens. Although it is still hot, the trees are preparing themselves for autumn. Already the leaves are gold and scarlet and what a riot of colours there will be in September! From the balcony we can see a huge glasshouse filled with palm trees, there are green lawns and avenues . . . only a few people come to the gardens, I haven't been there myself, yet. We shall go on Sunday.

Our house belongs to the Pharmaceutical Institute. Next door, behind high walls, is a hostel for girl students. Quite close, across the little river Karpovka, is the First Medical Institute, the former Petropavlovsky hospital, now renamed after Erisman. Erisman—a man of great heart and a clear mind, a scientist who did much for Russia.

The hospital and the First Medical Institute are like a small town, there are buildings of all shapes and sizes amongst the lovely trees of what was once an old church estate. Before the war I.D. was a professor at the Institute, and now he has been appointed Director.

Ketlinskaya, the secretary of the Leningrad Writers' Union, was glad to see me, and immediately telephoned the broadcasting service. I went straight there from the Union and it is arranged that I shall broadcast the next day.

27th August, 1941

The broadcast was called 'Moscow to Leningrad', and I began like this: 'Comrades, people of Leningrad! Citizens of the city of Lenin—I feel I want to convey to you my greetings from Moscow, from the city, which in these terrible days is as firm and as courageous as your Leningrad. We realise there, as you do here, the extent of the danger hanging over our country, but we are full of confidence that the danger will be overcome and the enemy beaten. Moscow and Leningrad, as brother and sister, stretch out their hands to each other, saying "Victory shall be ours".' I cited Herzen, who was brought up on stories of the burning of Moscow, the battle of Borodino, the victorious entry into Paris. How many future generations will look upon the present Moscow days as Herzen looked upon Napoleon's defeat! I finished by saying, 'Hitlerism will be destroyed, wiped off the face of the earth, and you, Moscow, my very own great capital, the heart of the Fatherland, the cradle of heroes—and you, Leningrad, the city bearing the name of Lenin, the pride and beauty of the country—you will stand invincible as you have stood down the centuries.'

A great many people have listened to this broadcast. My friend Olya Ch. heard it while she was queueing in a shop, and this is how she learned I am in Leningrad.

28th August, 1941

Today I.D. met a doctor he knows in one of the military hospitals that had been evacuated from Leningrad a week ago. All the week the patients and the equipment remained stationary on the train. It was unable to get away, and so it had to return to Leningrad.

The road to Mga—our last road to the outside world—has been cut by the Germans. Mga itself was taken a day or two after we passed through it.

1st September, 1941

We have ten or fifteen alerts each day. It seems more like one continuous alert with short breaks. But it is quiet—we do not even hear the anti-aircraft guns. Everything seems to be happening far away, beyond the horizon. We feel that the Junkers circle the outskirts of the city, but cannot break through . . . but the day will come when they will break through, as they did in Moscow.

And in spite of it all, or perhaps because of it, the Moscow sunsets were particularly beautiful. The sun was a great scarlet ball moving down towards the horizon. And as it sank, so the balloon barriage went up—as if a master mind was in charge of the whole operation.

Once there was an unforgettable moonrise; the moon was vast, filling all the window space. It was unnaturally pink and it looked waxen, the marks on the surface were like fingerprints— a great wax ball melting in hot hands.

I would take my typewriter and start down the stairs to the air-raid shelter. Once I met a woman on the stairs; she had gone out of her mind. Her husband was dead, but she thought he had stayed behind in the flat, alive. As she walked down, she cried, 'He was with me all the time, and then suddenly he lagged behind . . . how is he managing without his overcoat?'

I went on down. In the shelter there was a woman—a stranger to us—who was rushing to and fro in a frenzy, looking for her baby, asking if any of us had seen it. And all the time the baby was in her arms, wrapped in a shawl.

I never locked the door of my Moscow flat because of the danger of incendiary bombs. I was on the top floor, and, besides, the fire-watchers on the roof occasionally came for a drink of water.

Once I went up before the All Clear was sounded. Two of our tenants stood at the open window, speaking in low voices. Above the Kremlin walls the stars shone brilliantly; they shone with that particular brilliance we see in the hour before dawn, as if they are moist from dew. And in the distance the sky was scarlet from raging fires . . . the three of us stood for a long time watching the distant inferno.

4th September, 1941. Leningrad

I was at the editorial offices of our war newspaper when the editor and two of our Moscow writers and their driver returned from the front line. They came into the room, all of them wearing greatcoats and each had a hand-grenade behind his belt. The driver had four grenades and carried a portable machine-gun, which he put down on a table. One of the typists got up, and as she did, she shook the table, and the gun fell off with a clatter. What a mercy the safety catch was in place.

When they had put the grenades on the table the party unrolled a map and studied it with great attention. They were all very gloomy; their trip had been a failure, our troops have been pushed back, the Germans were bombing the Army H.Q. And they were all hungry.

Suddenly the telephone rang, and it was reported that one of our anti-aircraft batteries had shot down fifteen enemy planes . . . an unheard-of figure!

And all of them forget their gloom and their hunger, they pick up their grenades and their machine-gun and they rush out. They are to pay a visit to the battery.

5th September, 1941

A short report in the Leningrad Pravda on how the co-operative units work. The technical manager of one of the units went to the Board. He put a brand-new electric iron on the desk, and beside it he placed an unidentifiable object. 'We all esteem the iron,' he said. 'It is our business to make it. But now the Fatherland needs something different. We shall therefore cease the manufacture of this iron—the population will learn to live without it, for the time being—and we shall concentrate on this small object. We have discussed everything, weighed up the costs, so will you allow us to go ahead?' The Board allowed and now the team is manufacturing the small object. It is a tiny part of a rifle, but without it the rifle is a dead thing, and it cannot fire.

7th September, 1941

When the alert goes, one of our pharmaceutical students goes out on the landing and works our local siren. It looks like a coffee grinder and has a long handle . . . they are digging a line of trenches near Peterhof . . . of course the Germans will hit the fountains. . . .

I saw a German broadsword in the hands of a young Red Army man . . . talk about the spoils of war. . . .

8th September, 1941

We are having a wonderfully radiant autumn. There is no rain, and in this dry warmth the trees do not shed their leaves . . . and the leaves are turning amber yellow, lemon yellow, scarlet. . . .

I.D. spends the whole day at the Institute and I am alone in our high, over-light rooms. During alerts I go out on the balcony. Pesochnaya Street, which is always quiet, becomes completely deserted. Only air-raid wardens in their steel helmets stand looking up at the sky. Occasionally an apprentice craftsman will run along. Their hostel is in one of the buildings in the Botanical Gardens.

The woman tram driver had this to say about them: 'They carry on as if they owned the tram; hang on the step, push on the platform, but I don't mind any more. After all, they'll soon go off to the Front and dig trenches.'

One of our pilots parachuted straight into the arms of our girl students at the Medical Centre. He was slightly wounded. They were working on defence construction at the time. The fighting is quite near.

9th September, 1941

Yesterday—the first big air raid on Leningrad.

During the day there were a few alerts. Nevertheless we decided to go to the theatre—the Muskomediya, to see *The Flying Bat*. Nikolai Ivanovich Ozersky, his wife Alena and Fedya D. came with us. He is still the same Fedya to me, although he is now soon fifty and has a grand position as legal adviser to one of our ministries. He didn't leave, but remained in the city, preferring to stay in his well-loved flat, with its carpets, its books. . . .

Nikolai Ivanovich is I.D.'s deputy at the Institute. He is a shrewd, brainy man. His country accent is also very entertaining.

We had another alert in the interval. The manager came to speak to us in the foyer, and his manner was as casual as if he were announcing a change in the cast. He said clearly that he requested the citizens to stand as close to the walls as possible, inasmuch—and here he pointed to the dome—as there is very little protection overhead.

We obeyed and stood close to the walls for forty minutes. Somewhere in the distance anti-aircraft guns were firing. The play went on after the All Clear. The tempo was speeded up and the less important arias and duets were omitted.

There was still some daylight when we left the theatre. The blue dusk was mixed with reddish reflections and scarlet lights drifted along the square. Even then we did not understand what had happened.

Suddenly we saw our driver, Kovrov, making signs to us . . . but we had not ordered the car. Kovrov said, 'I decided to fetch you. The sooner you are home the better.' And his face, seen in the flares, was pale and troubled.

Then the car rounded the square, and suddenly we saw black, swirling mountains of smoke, illuminated from below by flames. All hell was let loose in the sky. Kovrov turned and said quietly, 'Some German dropped bombs and set the food stores on fire.'

There was one more alert as we drove. At home we stood for a long time on the balcony, watching the food stores go up in flames. At eleven we went to bed. But at two a.m. we had to go down to the shelter. (For the first time in Leningrad.) The German planes droned menacingly, directly over our heads. The anti-aircraft guns were never silent . . . so once again we heard the drone that was so familiar to us Muscovites.

The shelter is a long one, and there are benches along the wall. There is a loudspeaker on a shelf, and next to it a small first-aid cupboard. Women and children sat dozing on the benches. Conversations were held in whispers at the door, where the air-raid warden was on duty.

Suddenly a little boy ran the length of the shelter. He took a stool and dragged it to the wall by the loudspeaker. He climbed on the stool without any help, took the loudspeaker from the wall and pressing it to his ear listened for all he was worth . . . waiting for the longed-for words 'All Clear' to ring out.

10th September, 1941

The Badaev warehouses which have been burnt out were the central larder of Leningrad, the heart and stomach of the city.

And the sinister heavy smoke that hangs about in layers—that is burning sugar, flour, butter. . . .

For the last two weeks we have been spending our nights at the Institute. The night before last was warm, with brilliant moonlight. To the Germans, looking down from their planes, the city must have been as plain as the lines on the palm of one's hand.

Women orderlies are forbidden to run across the courtyard in their white gowns. The hospital buildings are white as well, as if they too wear gowns. But the buildings cannot be covered by a dark shawl wrapped round the shoulders.

The flashes of gun-fire from the anti-aircraft guns seem colourless in the brilliant moonlight. The searchlights are not needed. The Junkers come in waves, and they pass. It is quiet for a time, and then there is another wave. . . .

Yesterday I.D. wanted to see how the patients are lowered into the shelter. I went with him. As we came out of the Maternity Clinic we heard the whistle of a bomb. I was frightened. We ran. But the explosion occurred before we had time to reach the main building. I bent double, expecting the blast from the explosion. However, there was no blast—or it went in a different direction.

Later we were told in our H.Q. that a bomb fell near the Zoo, and that an elephant was buried under the debris . . . last night, bombs again and again on the same spot. The Germans are aiming at the chemical works, but they hit the Zoo. People say that all the monkeys are killed . . . and a maddened sable is roaming the streets . . . and how unbearably the dogs in the research department of the Institute howl during the raids. Poor creatures, they have the 'Pavlov' fistulae—as if that were not enough!

11th September, 1941

When the Germans entered Tallin, Vishnevsky, Tarasenkov and Braun were still able to contribute to the last issue of the *Leningrad Pravda*.

The break-through of the Baltic fleet from its encirclement was a desperate venture. German dive-bombers followed our ships relentlessly . . . military transports, destroyers, small craft—all moved under bombing attacks that went on day and night.

Those who got away with it the first time were generally hit the second or third voyage (Braun).

How good it is that Vishnevsky is here!

13 September, 1941

Yesterday evening, at about ten o'clock, we were trapped by army lorries outside the Botanical Gardens.

The moon had not yet risen, the night was close, dark and cloudy. The car came to take part of our belongings to the Institute, because we are now living there for at least half of the time.

While we were getting ready it became pitch dark. Lorries cluttered up our street, it was chaotic . . . they were parked lengthways, diagonally, across the pavement, bumper to bumper . . . and the commander of the convoy had disappeared.

For a second our driver switched on the headlights, and immediately a frenzied voice bellowed: 'Turn off your bloody lights. Switch them off.' And our driver replied: 'But I can't see a thing.'

At that moment the inevitable alert sounded, the sirens began to moan and wail in the dark, and at once, up in the low clouds, we heard the ominous droning. And there was nowhere we could escape . . . from back to front to side those lorries hemmed us in. We could hear them hitting against each other, crashing their sides. At last something in front of us began to move . . . we shifted a few yards . . . STOP! We were right up against the radiator of another car . . . again we started to back, scraped our wing on something, but in the end we moved off.

We turned left, along the Karpovka Quay. The driver said: 'I can't see the little bridge . . . we must be careful not to find ourselves in the water.'

That would be the last straw . . . We turned at random, and by chance we reached the bridge, where the Karpovka flows into the Nevka. Luckily we only scraped the railings. We drove along Leo Tolstoy Street, and once again the driver switched on our headlights, just for a second.

We were stopped by a patrol and asked if we have a night pass. We say yes, we have. It is true we have such a pass for the car. I, however, do not possess a night permit and it is after ten o'clock. At present the curfew is very strict.

We went further—we couldn't find the gates, so we turned on the lights again. A soldier appeared. 'If you turn on the lights once more, I shall fire.' He wasn't joking.

The journey took us about an hour, and the driver was half dead. He said, 'My shirt is drenched with sweat. It was such hell to drive.' We found it rather disturbing that such chaos can happen within the city itself.

Today's communiqué is bad. We have had to evacuate Chernigov. Artillery shells have begun to fall on the city. Last night three of them fell in Vereyskaya Street, next to the Obvodnoy Canal. This is worse than bombing—there is no warning—just death or injury out of the blue.

16th September, 1941

It gave me a strange feeling when the phone rang, and a fresh young voice said: 'The telephone is disconnected until the end of the war.' I tried to raise a protest, but knew in my heart it was useless. In a few minutes the phone clicked and went dead . . . until the end of the war.

And immediately the flat, too, became dead, frozen and tense. We were cut off from everyone and everything in the city. And that is how all the telephones in Leningrad were cut off at the same time. Only very special offices, clinics and hospitals are excepted.

17th September, 1941

A descendant of Pushkin came to visit me. Her grandmother was a cousin of Alexandr Sergeevich, and she herself is a true Hannibal* . . . black wavy hair, Ethiopian eyes, and thick lips which are an unusual shape when she smiles . . . . how strong this blood is!

Vera Kaetanovna is without a job, and she is unable to cope with life. The office she worked for has been evacuated, but for some reason she stayed behind. She has been given a pound of lentils, a piece of black bread and fifty roubles. Her daughter has fled from Pushkin from the Germans, and her son, a sick man, has taken to his bed and can't leave it. A relation of Pushkin fleeing from Pushkin from the Germans! Even a very experienced novelist might have difficulty dreaming that up.

* An Ethiopian called Hannibal was brought to Russia by Peter the Great and was an ancestor of Pushkin.

We have finally moved into the Institute, and into 'barrack-like conditions'. Our room is very small; there is a writing desk near the window, there are two iron beds, a small bookstand, one armchair and two small chairs. When we want to wash we have to carry in a washstand and basin. On the walls there are portraits of long-dead scientists—Claud Bernard, Bish, Pasteur, Wirhoff, Koch—and an engraving—'The English doctor Jenner giving the first smallpox vaccination to the eight-year-old James Phipps from the hand of the dairy-maid Sarah Nelms'.

We also have a circular iron stove, the little door facing the room. Efrosiniya Ivanovna gets it going, to take the chill off the room. There is a row of huge poplars in front of the window and we have persuaded ourselves that they will protect us from bomb and shell splinters. And the room is well placed in the wing joining the two main arms of the building.

This room is particularly good in the blackout, when total blackness falls on the city and on the hospital grounds. As we grope our way through this darkness, we somehow cannot believe that there is light anywhere in the world. Darkness, primordial darkness, confronts like a great wall. The sky itself is black, the moon is waning and dying now, and only appears with the dawn.

We make our way across the courtyard, passing the cold stone lobby of the main building. A small blue light is burning and the head porter sits reading a book. Guns are firing in the distance, and on the horizon the sky is ablaze. The planes are fighting up there.

The wounded are brought into the yard. One man was carried in yesterday, and all the way up the staircase blood dripped from the stretcher, from step to step. The stretcher was put down for a moment, and when it was lifted again there was a pool of blood on the ground. The casualty, a youngster, his face as white as paper, had come straight from the Front. He was taken at once to the operating theatre where his leg was amputated.

After passing through the courtyard with the wounded we go up the staircase and along a dark corridor, and then I enter our room where it is light and quiet. The window is blacked out, and a small lamp is burning on the desk. I brought this lamp from Moscow, and the pool of light it gives seems to me to be a sanctuary, a quiet paradise. To me, my room is a protection, a hearth, a home.

Of course, all this is illusory, but it is our illusions that help us to go on living.

Yesterday evening we went down to Casualty Ward. The raid was still on, and casualties were being admitted.

A young woman factory worker was waiting for an operation. She was seven months pregnant, and she was sitting in a steel chair, wrapped in a sheet. Her face was flushed with fever, her blue eyes were half closed, her fair hair, darkened with sweat, fell to her shoulders. The hospital gown was open at her breast.

The shell had hit her wooden workshop, and eighteen people out of twenty had been killed. She and one other worker were the sole survivors. She was shivering as she was lifted on to an operating table and anaesthetised. A splinter had gone deep into her leg, near the heel, and this was clearly seen on the X-ray.

The operation began, an incision was made in her leg, and eventually the splinter was pulled out with a pair of pincers.

But before that could be done, needles were used to locate the splinter, and when the splinter was found, it could not be pulled out at once, owing to the difficulty of getting a grip on it. In between bursts of anti-aircraft fire, we could hear the pincers scraping on the metal.

Ogloblina Zinaida Vasiliyevna was operating. She is one of our oldest doctors here. She studied when the Medical Institute was still the Women's Medical Institute, the first of its kind in Russia. She is inexhaustible, she doesn't go home for weeks on end, sometimes she stays at the operating table for twenty-four hours at a stretch.

We left before the operation finished, but later Boris Ykovlevich Shapiro (the hospital's chief physician) brought me the splinter, as I had asked him to do. It is a small fragment of metal, copper on the outside, steel on the inside.

Our Petrograd district of Leningrad is considered to be the safest. People from other parts of the city are being evacuated here. They are brought straight in on a tram, with just their immediate personal belongings—cradles, babies' baths, cooking utensils, books, even flowers.

Recently I travelled to Srednaya Rogatka nearly up to Pulkovo in an Isvestiya car. Pulkovo is right in the front line now, the Germans are almost there.

18th September, 1941

Yesterday I went to the Students' Hostel. It was dark, but there were two fires glowing in the sky. The Hostel is situated in the former barracks of the Grenadier Guards. Alexander Blok* used to live here. His stepfather was a soldier.

We are on the quiet banks of the Nevka, close to the Grenadiers' Bridge. There is a sunken barge in the water. The houses on the other side are reflected in the river. The colouring is pink and grey. This evokes the peace of a Dutch landscape. It reminds me, too, of that part of Copenhagen where the old granaries stand on the wharfside, and glossy doves peck at the grain as it spills . . . along the Nevka, to the left of the barracks, are our own familiar Botanical Gardens.

And the barracks themselves—a great old building, with thick, indestructible walls. The cellars are specially suitable for bomb shelters, though at this time the sole occupant is a half-wild cat . . . one thought, one question . . . will Leningrad be able to hold out?

19th September, 1941

The night was quiet—ominously so. It seemed that the city lay without breathing, in the darkness, waiting. And in the morning it started.

I listened on the radio to a talk by Ilya Ehrenburg on the Western Sector. It is a good talk, so is our position there . . . but here! It is really excellently spoken by Ehrenburg. 'Victory is usually depicted on wings, but really it is heavy footed. It creeps over land in a welter of mud and blood and is only gained at great cost.' That is the gist of his talk.

Oh, there are mine-fields, as it were, in my brain; places where I daren't tread, people I dare not think about, Jeanne and Mishenka,† for example. The wooden house in Peredelkino, amongst its firs and birch trees—this is another mine-field. Although I love the place, I couldn't be there now. I'd like to be at the Front, on the sector where we are advancing.

Every evening, here in the hospital, the badly wounded beg: 'Take us down to the shelter.' They are in a far worse state of nerves than patients who have not been in battle.

* Blok was one of the leading Russian poets of that time.
† Daughter and grandson of the author.

Outside there is the same golden autumn. The old trees drop their yellow leaves in the hospital avenues. Today another hospital is being moved here—a naval one.

Yesterday someone called our Petrograd region 'deep rear'. But if it is a 'rear' for the artillery, it isn't for the German planes. This morning is proof of it.

Bravery is as contagious as cowardice.

20th September, 1941

Yesterday was a bad day. There were many casualties, and many buildings were destroyed. All over the town we could hear a dull roar as a building collapsed.

We went by car to Razyeszhaya, to see Lelya P. Half an hour before we arrived two bombs fell, one in the road between the houses along the Bolshaya Moskovskaya, another in the courtyard. Lelya's house was damaged by both bombs. The house next door had a direct hit, and killed and wounded were being carried out from the ruins.

The courtyard was strewn with glass and bricks; in the flat itself the floor was covered with plaster, dirt and lime, just as if it were being redecorated. And in the room next door, where Lelya's mother, Dina Osipovna, had been sitting, the stove collapsed in a great heap of debris. The flat is in a terrible state.

Lelya and I come from the same place—Odessa. We have known each other almost from childhood. I remember her in the autumn of 1913 in Paris. She was so young, so gay, so attractive. A whole crowd of us went off to some fair. We rode on the roundabouts, and ate chestnuts, looking at Paris through falling leaves as the lights of early evening came on.

Now Lelya has a daughter—Inna—a pretty, serious-minded young girl. She dreams of becoming a navigating officer in a ship, and of travelling to distant places.

When we arrived at the Razyeszhaya, Lelya was at work. Dina Osipovna met us, clambering over the debris.

Today we met a major who had flown in from Moscow; he was flying back there the same day. He told us about Zhukov, and as we parted, he said, 'Leningrad will remain in our hands. Surrender would be impossible.' He explained why, and although we knew it already, and had talked about it scores of times, and thought about it endlessly, to hear this from someone who had been near the battle of Yelnya gave us new heart. And God how we need it!

Yesterday more hospitals were set on fire by incendiary bombs. The Kuibyshevsky, the Alexandrovsky and two other military hospitals. We could see smoke like burning crude oil pouring from the military hospital on the Sovietsky Prospekt.

Yesterday, too, bombs were dropping in the Novaya Derevnya, on the market place. Fifty people were brought in, one of them a child of about seven years old. She kept complaining that the rubber tourniquet on her leg was hurting her. People comforted her, telling her that the pain would soon be easier. Then she was anaesthetised, and her leg amputated. She came round and said, 'Everything is marvellous. It doesn't hurt any more.' She had no idea she had lost her leg.

22nd September, 1941

We have lost Kiev. I am sick at heart. There were a few alerts yesterday afternoon. We went into town. An alert. We dropped into the Oserskys' to wait for the All Clear. They live in the former palace of Cyril Razumovsky. The rooms are high, huge and cold. Everything belongs to another age—the eighteenth century. And over the palace we have the twentieth century—a Junkers, laden with bombs.

Today we went to town to see 'T' at the offices of the newspaper of the Baltic Fleet. We had just arrived when there was an alert. A sailor appeared and said, 'Everyone is ordered to go down to the shelter.'

We moved down the corridor, and at that moment the house shook. A bomb had fallen next door, in the Apraksin market.

In a shelter, in a corner under the vaults, built by Rossi, 'T' spread out his greatcoat. We sat down and from his pocket he pulled out a bundle of letters from his wife and began to read them to me. And it was astounding, incredible, to hear such words of love and tenderness beneath the sound of explosions and the drone of bombers.

We drove home without waiting for the All Clear. As we got back to the Institute, we were told that the Students' Hostel, in the Grenadier Guards' barracks, had had a direct hit about twenty minutes ago. So off we rushed to the barracks.

We drove towards it, looking out with great anxiety. Is the building still standing? It is. Only some windows are without glass. The bomb was a small one and fell in the courtyard, the crater had already filled up with muddy water. But even such a small bomb had caused the building to crack, and plaster had fallen on the students' beds. If anyone had been lying on a bed at that moment he would not have lived to tell the tale.

I am moved by the thought that while the bombs rain down on this besieged city Shostakovich is writing a symphony. *Leningrad Pravda*'s report on it is tucked away between communiqués of the southern front and reports of petrol bombs. And so, in all this horror, art is still alive. It shines and warms the heart.

23rd September, 1941

In the Pushkarskaya Street I saw a house that had been sliced in two from attic to cellar. There it stands, cracked right through, its roof half off, and looking like the crust of a partly baked loaf. As we passed this house we saw that a sofa was being lowered by a rope from the sixth floor. It made its way slowly downwards, balancing over the void.

The Germans have learned to use a new techhique. First of all they drop high-explosive bombs, then, when the building is shattered and vulnerable, they follow it up by dropping incendiaries. This is what has happened in the military hospital, where many of the wounded perished.

Today our chief doctor received an order—a stretcher must be placed by the bed of each dangerously ill patient, and rope ladders must be in each ward.

We have an uncomfortable neighbour in the Grenadier Barracks. Only part of the barracks is assigned to the Students' Hostel, the Army is housed in the other buildings. Live shell cases are often transported there (alas, not frequently enough). Sometimes they are delivered by tram, sometimes by barge along the river Karpovka. There is an anti-aircraft battery there as well, on the quiet river bank, not far from our mortuary. The Germans observe all this from above.

A blimp is hidden amongst the trees, opposite, complete with its spare cylinder. This is a dangerous neighbourhood for a hospital—and as for the hospital itself—well, we know how the Germans treat them with very special care.

However—after the youngster had shown me the bomb crater, and the place where he had been standing, and said,

'I was there,' it dawned on me that there is nothing anyone can do to be safe . . . it's all a matter of chance. We can try to avoid standing near windows but that's about all.

24th September, 1941

Today it is a wonderful morning, all golden. At about half past ten, and a few seconds before the alert, a bomb fell in our grounds and did not explode. It is still here, embedded in the earth. It fell next to the Polyclinic, close to the iron fountain. The Sappers have worked on it all day, but they can't get down to it. So they have left it till tomorrow. It is a very large bomb; this can be seen from a piece of the stabiliser which broke off. The maternity ward and the first surgical ward were nearest to the bomb, but they have been moved to other premises.

The strange thing is that I hardly felt the impact. My first reaction was that a heavy door had banged. The building trembled, but not very much. People say that the shock was greater in other blocks.

Lelya, with Dina Osipovna and Inna, have moved from their bombed-out flat to us in the Pesochnaya. Now I shall go there often.

Every day I go to the second surgical ward to read to the wounded. I have two wards there, and I read Gorky, Nekrasov and Twain. Stories by Mark Twain and Nekrasov's *Who is living well in Russia* are very popular.

Some of the most badly wounded are either semi-conscious or too ill to follow any thoughts but their own. Nevertheless, it pleases them that someone comes and talks to them. They speak with bitterness about the German expertise, and about the fact that we haven't sufficient guns and aircraft. One soldier mutters over and over again, in a scarcely audible whisper: 'Darling tanks are what we need, darling tanks, beloved tanks. . . .' Another officer, who lost a leg at Kingisepp, said: 'I am willing to be wounded again if only we could win the war.' A third soldier, who had a medal for bravery touchingly pinned to his nightshirt, says, 'If only they'd drive off these locusts.' He means the German planes. A fourth soldier was rambling on about trenches and dugouts. 'They do not leave our earth in peace.'

26th September, 1941

The wounded are quiet enough during the alerts, but they get very depressed, and this is because they realise how helpless they are. After all, most of them are incapable of moving a single step.

A few days ago I was sitting on a stool in the middle of the ward, reading aloud a story by Gorky. Suddenly the sirens began to wail; the sound of anti-aircraft fire seemed to fill the entire sky, a bomb crashed, the windows rattled.

I sat on my stool, unable to lean back, as there was nothing to lean back against . . . surrounded by windows, and by the wounded—those helpless people, all looking towards me— who alone was well and mobile. I summoned up all my will-power. I let the drone of the aircraft go past, and then I read on, anxious lest my voice should shake with fear. But when I got home I felt so weak with fear and I had to go and lie down for a little while.

The soldiers know about our unexploded bomb, but they mention it only casually. Do they realise that it is still there, and still unexploded?

27th September, 1941

The bomb is still there. The bomb-disposal squad are working themselves to a standstill. But it is like some deeply hidden treasure that won't give up its secrets, it buries itself deeper and deeper into the ground. What work they manage to do during the day is all undone at night. The earth has been dug up all over our garden. 'They do not leave our earth in peace.'

28th September, 1941

A meeting of the Women of Leningrad took place today. Vasilyeva (the editor of *Smena*) and I sat up all night at her place, writing the address. During the inevitable raid neigh-bours from the upper floors came down to us. They sat dole-fully with their children in the entrance hall, under the coat rack. For some reason, none of them went down to the shelter.

It is far more frightening to be in a raid in someone else's house than it is to be in one's own.

29th September, 1941

The bomb is still there. Already we have almost forgotten it, but it is still dangerous.

4th October, 1941

In order to prevent the bomb from burrowing any deeper it was necessary to build the sort of wooden support, used in mining, to prevent it sinking. Today at last we were called to look at the monster. Part of the garden has been cordoned off, and nobody has been allowed to go inside this cordon, but now I.D. and I were allowed to go.

The whole high-explosive bomb was there, exposed, clearly visible. It was enormous, the body painted a bluish colour, the firing mechanism yellow. It had a tapering snout and a blunt rear.

The detonator was unscrewed and moistened with water. This was done by putting the water on the end of a long spade. Then a greenish clay was dug out. It looked harmless, but it was 'Trotil'—the actual explosive. Now the bomb has been moved to the War Museum, and we have kept a piece of the stabiliser as a souvenir.

5th October, 1941

I cannot get that bomb out of my head. I am starting to write a poem about it in the same metre as my *Travel Diary*.

I have received a letter from Chistopol, dated August 18th. Jeanne writes about the boy, 'He is much thinner, but he is growing. He is already eating porridge and jelly.' What a wonderful thing it is that they are there.

10th October, 1941

We have had to evacuate Orel. As before, things are very threatening in the Vyasma and Briyansk sectors. The Germans are advancing again.

Near Moscow, the country is flat, there are no mountains or valleys or sea. How on earth can the horde of tanks be held in such terrain? It makes my blood run cold when I think of them trampling through the streets of Moscow.

14th October, 1941

Heavy fighting near Odessa. It's so long since I left it. I thought it meant no more to me than any other place, that I had almost no feeling for it as my native town. But now it is different, and I feel that it is as near and dear to me as it used to be.

I wrote a poem called 'Salute to Odessa'. I shall probably broadcast it tomorrow, so that the people of Odessa will be able to listen to it.

15th October, 1941

I was too late. The Germans are in Odessa.

26th October, 1941

I went to the Philharmonic Hall. Kamensky played Tchaikovsky's Piano Concerto and gave the Prater Valse as an encore. Already the concert hall has lost its festive look. It isn't heated and I had to keep on my coat. There were a lot of soldiers in the audience.

5th November, 1941

I have to force myself to read about the fighting near Moscow. The Germans are so near the city. Today the *Leningrad Pravda* printed a despatch—'Fighting on the Mozhaisk Highway'. We have driven on this highway so many times. And now the German tanks are rumbling along it, and the German infantry is marching . . . now a new sector has appeared in the news— Maloyaroslavl, the town of N. [apparently Nara]. Suburban trains used to go there, stopping at Peredelkino on the way . . . the Germans will not get to Moscow, such a thing cannot happen.

> 'Moscow, it cannot be but Russian
> As man cannot live and not breathe.'

6th November, 1941

Yesterday, for the first time in my life, I understood the expression 'My legs gave way'. I was alone on a large, resounding staircase, by a landing with a huge window, when a bomb crashed nearby. There was the familiar thunderclap—and then came the rumbles . . . the ground shook, like an earthquake, it trembled as if it were water, and then the house began to shake.

I was out of my mind with fear, and I ran to the shelter, which was already full of people. My legs felt as if they were made of cotton wool. Later this feeling passed.

This was the closest shave I had during the entire war. In many parts of our building glass was blown out of the windows. This happened in our wing, too, but not in our room. We are indeed well situated.

The shelter of the command point of our institute and hospital is in a small room. It is separated from the large shelter by a partition. There is a table in the centre, and people sit round it, reading, sewing and following the fighting on the war maps. There is a small stove in the corner, and two settees against the walls. There is an internal telephone connecting I.D. and Boris Yakovlevich with all the departments.

The sound of bomb explosions only reaches us here indistinctly. If a dull thud is heard, it means that the bomb has not exploded at once. We sit, therefore, and count the seconds. . . .

While the raids are on, my friend Marietta (Mariya Ignatieyevna Palchevskaya) sits doing embroidery. When a delayed-action bomb falls, and we wait for the explosion, her needle remains suspended in mid-air, and when the bomb explodes the work goes on smoothly.

Marietta is a pharmacologist. Her department is on the same floor as ours, and the odour of guinea-pigs and rabbits lingers. Indeed, the cages still stand in the corridor, but the guinea-pigs and the rabbits are no longer there.

Our anti-aircraft gunners have a sheep-dog called Dinka. Usually, she lies in front of the shelter, quivering with apprehension. The Commander is in touch with a high observation post on the roof of our anatomy theatre, by phone, and with all other observation posts in the district. He receives information from all of them about the approach and direction of the German planes, and it is he who directs the fire. We talk in whispers, so as not to disturb the Commander.

But in spite of the daily, hourly danger, despite the fact that I don't know whether I shall see Jeanne and the boy again, despite ill health, despite everything, it is a long time since my morale has been so high, or since I have had such an urge to work. I can do a great deal now, and do it I shall, so long as no bomb falls closer than the one that fell yesterday. If I remain alive I shan't let unimportant, irrelevant things get in the way. All I want is to keep a clear head so that I am able to write to the very end. That is all I wish for myself.

7th November, 1941

Yesterday we listened to Stalin's speech from Moscow.

We decided that for this occasion we must warm up the ice-cold room a little. But it proved impossible, and we sat in our overcoats. Nevertheless the little heap of coals in the stove glowed with heat and light. We couldn't keep our eyes off it.

And the night outside was pitch dark, black with the sirens wailing and the barking of the guns and the sound of the planes droning overhead.

Twice the alerts went, and Stalin's speech was immediately relayed again. It came across above the darkness, above the alerts, above the raid. It was stronger than anything.

We listened to it, as we stared at the fire, and everything merged for us as one great shining consolation.

10th November, 1941

Yesterday we went to the Philharmonic Hall to hear Beethoven's Ninth Symphony. I'm afraid it looks as if there will be no more concerts for us. It is getting too complicated and dangerous.

On our way home the night was so black it was like being inside a room without a light. We had no torch, and we reached the tram-stop by miracle. We were nearly run over by lorries. At one moment I could feel the cold wet edge of a lorry right against my cheek.

The Philharmonic Hall gets increasingly gloomy. The cold is arctic. The bread ration has been reduced for the second time.

15th November, 1941

Yesterday a large high-explosive bomb fell next to the mortuary. A second fell in the Botanical Gardens. All the glass in the hot-houses was blown out, and cold air rushed in. And in the morning all the palms were dead.

When the first bomb fell, the door of our shelter shook as violently as if some terrified person was trying to pull it open. I rushed to open it. I couldn't believe it was the effect of blast. I threw open the door and no one was there. Dinka the sheep-dog lay trembling on the floor, and the women sitting motionless pressed their children tighter to themselves.

16th November, 1941

An alert. Many flares. At night the whole of our area is flooded with light.

21st November, 1941

Yesterday, as we were coming back from town, we got into two big raids. Twice we went into shelters, twice we sheltered in doorways; in the breaks in between we did what is known as 'running across'. As soon as things quieten down a little, we go on our way. When the guns start to blaze and the planes are overhead, we wait. Spiky red stars of exploding anti-aircraft shells look very menacing in the darkness. Their fragments are very dangerous.

The first alert caught us at the Stock Exchange Building. There was a murky white haze, everything looked ghostly through the driving snow. The Rostalny columns were hardly visible. And over all this, the wail of the sirens, the thud of a bomb somewhere near.

We went down to the cellar under the Stock Exchange, down to the mighty ancient vaults. The tram driver and the conductor (both women) came with us, and we were pleased because it meant that the tram wouldn't go without us!

The second shelter, in the large building in the Bolshoi Prospekt, was quite different. A queue was waiting for soya milk in another part of the building, and it descended with us *en masse*. And it so happened that two workers of a sweet factory of pre-revolutionary days met there, a man and a woman. He had been a pastry cook there. One of those things that just had to happen.

They started reminiscing about the old days. The former cook told us about the 'chocolate gospel' that his factory had made for the Paris Exhibition, and for which the factory owner received a prize of 25,000 roubles. He gave a mere pittance to the workers who had made it. But the most interesting thing, according to the ex-cook, was that the Paris judges had accepted the 'gospel' as having been made with pure cream butter, while, in fact, it happened to have been made with margarine.

What 'sweet' recollections indeed! Everyone in the shelter

listened spellbound, paying little attention to the sounds of the raid outside.

In Tolstoy Square we were running under a barrage of fire when suddenly, by the baker's shop on the corner of that icy place, we heard a trembling plea:

'My darlings, my dear ones, help!' An old woman had fallen down in the darkness. Planes droned in the sky above her, fires raged round her, and in the Square not a soul except ourselves. We put her on her feet again, and we were on the point of going off when she pleaded:

'My darlings, my children, I have lost my bread-ration cards. What shall I do without them? My dears, help me . . .' And she fumbled in the darkness for her pensioner's hundred-gramme cards.

I was overcome by fear and exhaustion, and I had reached the end of my tether. I said, 'Look for yourself. We cannot.'

I.D. said nothing. He let go of my arm, bent down, searched around and found the old woman's ration cards. Later we led her to Petropavlovskaya Street, and then we ran for home.

25th November, 1941

Yesterday, while firing was going on in the air and from the ground, Boris Yakovlevich (our hospital chief) faced the learned Council, defending his thesis, in the shelter.

He arrived wearing, as usual, his quilted jacket. He had come straight from the boiler room. He and the boiler man had spent several days getting the laundry in working order after it had been damaged by a shell.

Electricity isn't working in the shelter. The Scientific Council held the meeting with a paraffin lamp. At dinner we drank diluted spirits in honour of the new 'Candidate of Medical Sciences'.

An old woman prays for the lifting of the blockade. 'Lord, hammer a way through to our soldiers.'

28th November, 1941

The aerial migration of Leningrad goes on. Quite a number of our writers have been flown out, and amongst those connected with the Institute Professors Z. and K. have gone too. It isn't a simple matter at all; there is fear for the future and love of the city (how can anyone leave it at such a moment!). And also the realisation that you wouldn't be evacuated unless the country needed you. And how can you resist flying away if you are offered the chance?

The future of Leningrad fills me with anxiety. The burning of the Badayev Stores was no joke. Fat going up in heavy smoke— the carbohydrates necessary to maintain life. Protein—meat— we hardly see at all. Recently Professor Z. told me, 'Yesterday my daughter spent all day in the attic searching for the cat.' I was prepared to be deeply touched by such love for animals, but Z. added: 'We eat them.'

Another time, Professor Z., a passionate hunter, said, 'My life will come to an end when I shoot my last blackcock, and I'm rather afraid that I have shot him.'

Already, in November, there have been two reductions in the bread ration—two definite steps downwards.

30th November, 1941

Beethoven's Fifth Symphony to be given in the Philharmonic Hall was cancelled in view of a strong artillery bombardment.

1st December, 1941

Today in Wulf Street we saw a corpse on a small sleigh. There was no coffin. It was wrapped in a white shroud, and the knees were clearly discernible; the sheet was bound tightly round. A biblical, ancient Egyptian burial. The shape of a human form was clear enough, but one couldn't tell whether it was of a man or a woman. It had become merely a body belonging to earth.

6th December, 1941

Jeanne writes: 'The boy has become so lovely. He is a joy to behold. As soon as we move, and regain our senses a little, I will try to take a photograph of him and send it to you.'

7th December, 1941

Beethoven's Fifth Symphony and Tchaikovsky's Overture 1812. The Philharmonic Hall is becoming increasingly sombre and hellishly cold. The chandeliers burn only a quarter of their power. Some members of the orchestra wear quilted jackets and some wear half-length sheepskin coats. As violinists need to keep their hands and arms free, and cellists even more so, they wear the quilted coats. The double basses can wear the sheepskin coats, as their movements are directed downwards. The drummer has the best of it. He warms himself by striking blows on his drums. The leader was badly shaven. Probably he lacked the means to heat up water or had no light to see by.

Yesterday there was an important announcement on the radio. England has declared war on Hungary, Rumania and Finland.

8th December, 1941

Japan has attacked America without declaring war.

9th December, 1941

We breathe . . . we breathe a little deeper . . . we have occupied Tikhvin. Maybe the Salvation of Leningrad will begin from here.

11th December, 1941

Things are going well near Moscow. Moscow has repelled the Germans, but at Leningrad the position is still threatening.

Today shells have been falling along the Kirov Prospekt. The shelling caught us as we were approaching our house. A shell burst at the main gateway, just as we were driving up at the front door, and were about to get out of the car.

The whole street was enveloped in a powdery smoke which gave off a sour kind of smell. Our water mains and the link with the main sewage system have been damaged. Now we are without water.

Near the entrance gate there is a large iced-up crater, the pavement is covered with ice and frozen rivulets radiate a long way out.

14th December, 1941

Success near Volkhov again.

21st December, 1941

Yesterday I decided to pay a visit to Evgeniya Osipovna P. Is she alive? Is her husband alive? They are great friends of mine. She is head of the Teaching Faculty in the Herzen Institute. At present she is working in their hospital as a sister. She works very hard; her skin is yellow, her eyes have become dim and her grey hair and her little old fur hat seem to merge into one.

The trams are unpunctual and irregular now. Many lines are damaged. But we decided to go by tram at least part of the way. So along we went through Bolshoi Prospekt to Vedenskaya Street, and boarded the tram for route 12. It wasn't our route, but at least it would take us over the bridge, which, after all, was the main thing.

We had hardly started when the shelling began. Shells fell to right and left of us. There was a roaring sound—the street was an inferno. The crashes reverberated as if we were at the bottom of a canyon.

No one in the tram said a word.

We were carried into the actual zone of fire. The most frightening part was to see people on the pavement running away from the very place we were approaching, getting nearer every moment.

Suddenly the woman driver said, 'I'm not going any further. I'm afraid.' Everyone shouted at her, 'Don't stop! Go ahead, we shall rush through it.' At first she obeyed and we hurtled past one stop like a whirlwind. But at the next stop (Sitnoy Market) a shell fell so close that the driver let go of the wheel and the tram stopped.

I can no longer remember how—but we managed to jump out of the tram, run across the street and into the baker's shop on the corner. And at the very moment we entered the shop a shell hit our tram.

We must have spent nearly an hour in the baker's shelter. I don't remember just how long, because I became terribly sleepy. This always happens to me in times of danger, or soon afterwards.

The shelter was damp, water dripped from above. All the time people were moving about in search of a drier place. A child was crying. And I was uncontrollably sleepy, I would have given a year of my life for a pillow!

When things quietened down, we went out. Our tram stood there, smashed to pieces. It was petrifying. Someone pointed to it and said: 'It's full of bodies.'

Everyone who had stayed in that tram was killed.

When we reached home we learned that the shelling had been deliberately aimed at Sitnoy Market, into the thick of the Sunday shopping crowd. Seventy-two wounded were brought into our hospital.

22nd December, 1941

Ten people out of the seventy-two died.

25th December, 1941

This morning when our Efrosiniya Ivanovna brought in the firewood I could see at once by the look on her face that something extraordinary had happened. She told me that just before dawn she went to the baker's and in Leo Tolstoy Square she saw a man laughing, crying, clutching his head as he walked along.

'He'd stand still for a little while, and then move on a few steps as if he didn't know what he was doing. I thought, Either he has had one too many—and wherever did he manage to get hold of it?—or he's out of his mind.'

And only when she reached the baker's shop did Efrosiniya Ivanovna understand what had happened. The bread ration has been increased, and this man was one of the first to learn about it. The radio doesn't work for lack of current, the newspapers are only posted on the walls every second or even third day. Therefore, people only learned that the bread ration had gone up when they were at the counter. That's what happened to the stranger and also to Efrosiniya Ivanovna. Everyone is radiant. The same thing is heard everywhere. 'They've increased it!'

Manual workers now receive 250-300 grammes, white-collar workers 250 grammes. I.D. and I will have 600 grammes a day for the two of us.

26th December, 1941

It is frightening when we leave in the morning by our rear gates. Outside is our mortuary, on the banks of the Karpovka, and this has now become the mortuary for the entire district.

Each day, eight to ten bodies are brought there on sleighs. And they just lie on the snow. Fewer and fewer coffins are available, and less and less material to make them. So the bodies are wrapped in sheets, in blankets, in tablecloths, sometimes even in curtains. Once I saw a small bundle wrapped in paper and tied with string. It was very small, the body of a child.

How macabre they look on the snow! Occasionally, an arm

or a leg protrudes from the crude wrappings. In these multi-coloured rags there still lingers a semblance of life, but there is also the stillness of death. This makes me think of a battle-ground and a doss-house at the same time.

The mortuary itself is full. Not only are there too few lorries to go to the cemetery, but, more important, not enough petrol to put in the lorries . . . and the main thing—there is not enough strength left in the living to bury the dead.

The question has arisen about not registering every individual death any longer. And in order to simplify formalities, a representative of the Registry will be present in the mortuary, just to count the number of bodies. After all, there are so many nameless ones.

30th December, 1941

Recently, at one place, twenty-seven powders of ascorbic acid (Vitamin C) were exchanged for a live dog. (The dog to be eaten.) Marietta said, reasonably, 'Why not, if the dog is a large one? It is a profitable exchange.'

1st January, 1942

Yesterday we saw the New Year in twice. The first time was at five o'clock in the evening, at the Writers' Union. First articles and poetry were read out, and later we ate a supper, paid for by coupons cut out of our ration cards.

We walked to the Union through icy, deserted streets. Past the tram depot, from which no tram leaves, past the bakery which gives us so little bread, past a bus riddled with shrapnel, and buried in the snow. Along the quay where two unfinished ships are berthed, tragic and silent; in front of them, the icy bulk of the city; behind, the frozen Neva.

In the Writers' Union the reading took place in the red drawing room. Small logs were burning in the open fire, there was a candle on the table. It was very cold.

My turn came. I moved nearer to the candle and began to read from the manuscript of the first stanza of a poem (I have not yet decided on a title). I was reading it in public for the first time. When I got to the part where I curse Germany, I could hardly breathe. I had to stop and start again three times.

After 'supper' we went home by the same route. It was quite dark.

In the evening, I.D. went to the baker's. He was caught on his way back by the alert. Once again bombs were falling close to the Square. I.D. sheltered in a gateway, with the bread. I, waiting at home, was very very worried about him.

By midnight we went down to the Medical Superintendent's consulting room. We took down our last bottle of Riesling, which had gone sour. We poured the wine into glasses, but the house telephone rang. The doctor on duty reported from Casualty that he had forty bodies lying in corridors, even in the bathroom. He was at a loss to know what to do next. So the Medical Superintendent went to Casualty, and we went to our room and to bed.

2nd January, 1942

Most of the people admitted to the hospital die in Casualty. Long trenches are dug in the cemetery, in which the bodies are laid. The cemetery guards only dig separate graves if they are bribed with bread.

There are many coffins to be seen in the streets. They are transported on sleighs. If the coffin is empty it moves easily from side to side, it skids. Once such a coffin hit my legs. A coffin with a body is usually pulled by two women. The ropes cut deeply into their shoulders, but not because the coffin is heavy; rather because the women are weak.

Recently I saw a body without a coffin. It had on the chest, under the twisted shroud, some wood shavings, apparently as a mark of dignity. One felt a professional not an amateur hand. This technical touch was more macabre than anything. It could well be that this had to be paid for by bread.

Another time, two sleighs caught by their runners. On one sleigh a spade and a crowbar were neatly tied to the lid of the coffin. The other sleigh carried logs. Truly a meeting of life and death.

Living people are frequently carried on sleighs as well. I saw two women pulling a sleigh with some difficulty. A third woman sat on it. She was holding a dead child wrapped in a small blanket. This was by the Anichkov Bridge, where Klodt's bronze horses used to be, before they were removed to a safer place.

The other day I saw an emaciated, though still young, woman having trouble with her sleigh. For on it she had put a large so-called 'modern' wardrobe from a Commission shop, and this was to be converted into a coffin.

One Sunday we walked from our gate to the Leo Tolstoy Square, and on this small stretch we met eight coffins, large and small, and a few bodies which were carried wrapped in blankets. At the same time two women were leading a third to our hospital, she being at the start of her labour. There were dark bags under her eyes—sure sign of scurvy. She was as thin as a skeleton and was hardly able to drag one foot after the other.

On another occasion I saw two women who looked like teachers or librarians pulling an old man along on a sleigh. He wore spectacles, an overcoat and a fur hat, and he lay uncomfortably on the small sleigh, leaning on his elbow, his legs dragging on the ground. 'Be careful! Do be careful!' he cried at every pothole. And those women were sweating profusely, in spite of forty degrees of frost.

Two more women were leading a man with muscular distrophy (we have learned of the illness only here). His legs, in high felt boots, moved like artificial limbs, his eyes stared madly, as if he were possessed. The skin on his face was tightly stretched, the lips, half open, revealed teeth which seemed enlarged from hunger. His nose, sharpened as if it had melted, was covered with small sores, and the tip had bent slightly sideways. Now I know what is meant by 'gnawed by hunger'.

Faces one sees in the street are either unnaturally drawn and shiny (dropsical swellings) or green and lumpy. There is not an ounce of fat under the skin. And these desiccated skeletons are being gnawed by frost. (As I write these words I can hear a mouse, crazy with hunger, rummaging in the waste-paper basket, into which we used to throw crumbs. We call her Princess Myshkina. She hasn't even the strength to rejoice that all the cats have been eaten.)

I cannot stand the sharp, penetrating smell of pine extract. It means either that a lorry has passed carrying corpses soaked in this fluid, or that an empty lorry (usually a gas-driven one) is passing, having delivered its load. This deathly smell stays suspended in the frosty air.

Evening

This morning, when we were on our way to the icy canteen for our lunch, a man was brought to us. He was an acquaintance of Boris Yakovlevich, possibly a doctor himself. He came to beg us to admit his starving wife to hospital, and while he was begging on her behalf he fainted from hunger and it was he who was carried past us into Casualty.

And yesterday we saw a stranger in a corner by the door. He was sitting on a chair by the key cupboard, where the duty nurse usually sits. His head was sunk on his chest, and his arms dropped lifelessly at his sides. All his muscles sagged, one of his galoshes had dropped by the chair.

B.Y. touched his temple, on the spot where a small muscle throbbed, and said, 'There are faint signs of life.'

After numerous telephone calls, exhausted orderlies arrived and carried the man into Casualty. Whether he is still alive, nobody knows. He was a workman in a nearby factory. He had been given a medical certificate and was on his way to hospital. He walked through the main entrance which is now so superficially guarded, managed to reach the chair and quietly began to die, as thousands of these dystrophics are dying—sunk in an icy void.

3rd January, 1942. Evening

The man we saw yesterday on a stretcher wasn't a doctor but a physicist. He died in Casualty about half an hour after his admission. The man who sat in the corner under the key cupboard had died, too.

Our position at the front near Moscow is excellent. Leningrad is living at the expense of the last remnants of its strength. This ultimate effort can be felt everywhere. There are no trams. Exhausted people walk several kilometres daily, sometimes over ten. In making this effort they are using up their last calories.

In many of the town's districts (in ours as well) there is no radio, in order to save power. Plumbing functions only on the lower floors, and not always then. What will it be like in the spring when the snow melts?

Petrol tanks were to have been delivered to the town today, but none turned up. There was no coal for the railway engine.

People say (and it is true) that everywhere—in Tikhvin, in Volkhov, in Murmanskk—particularly in Murmanskk—train loads of food supplies are waiting. People talk about it with rapture, greed, tenderness. Some don't talk at all; they haven't enough strength left.

The word is that there's everything up to and including bananas. I heard about bananas for the first time in our canteen where the walls are quite fuzzy with hoar frost, and where the temperature is well below zero. Bananas!

Militia-men* are brought into Casualty. They die before they even have time to warm up.

Once a girl engineering student picked up a militia-man who had fallen down from hunger. His ration card had been stolen as well. The girl dragged the man on to her back, pulled him to a baker's and bought him the next day's ration with a coupon from her own card. And how will she fare next day?

The blackout has become very careless, maybe because there have been no raids for some time, maybe from sheer weakness. Blinds are lowered carelessly. After all, there is practically no electricity. Frost covers the windows with icy shields.

Up in the sky, the moon gives a savage, frenzied green light which eclipses our little paraffin lamps on earth.

There were rejoicings on the day the bread ration was increased by seventy-five grammes, but that was a long time ago. People have forgotten about it now, and the man who walked laughing and crying towards our Efrosiniya Ivanovna probably died a long time ago too. Efrosiniya herself is hardly alive. Her husband is dying. He used to be a chef. In his semiconscious state he is haunted by visions of dishes prepared by him in bygone days. Pommes souflés, bœuf Stroganoff . . . sauces . . . their aroma, their appearance in the sizzling butter in the pan . . . and so he rambles on about it, torturing himself and everyone around him. Efrosiniya cries and says, 'He will be the death of me.'

What will happen if no food supplies are brought in during the immediate future? The winter will go on for a long time yet . . . a terrible winter.

At present our nights are indescribably quiet—not a hooter, nor the sound of a tram, nor the bark of a dog, nor the mew of a

---

* Militia in the Soviet Union are equivalent to police.

cat. There is no radio. The city falls asleep in dark icy flats, many never wake up.

I have had no letter from the family in Chistopol for a long time. But how can any letters batter their way through to here?

4th January, 1942

Last night a fire broke out in the Students' Hostel; an ill-fated place which has already been hit twice by bombs.

At first it was assumed that the fire was caused by a make-shift stove put in the wrong place, but later it became clear that it was caused by a match thrown into a corner, on to a heap of rubbish—whether inadvertently or on purpose, who knows? It could have been the latter, because in the commotion caused by the fire things began to disappear.

One of the firemen worked particularly well in the smoke, and without a mask. There was no oxygen. It was decided to give him a reward. He, however, when he learned he had been fire-fighting in a medical building, said, 'I don't want any reward except maybe a hundred grammes of fish oil for my wife.' And he received the precious oil, so rich in vitamins.

Our mouse (Princess Myshkika) has become very quiet— apparently for ever. It's a pity. There was some kind of life when this tiny bundle moved, but now it can't be there any more.

It seems to me that unless the blockade is broken within the next ten days the city cannot hold out . . . Leningrad has had all it can take from this war—the Germans should get back as good as they have given in full measure.

The USSR is being called the Saviour of Mankind, and indeed it is so.

I am proud to possess a Soviet passport. It is a modest document, olive-green in colour, nevertheless to me it gives out a sort of radiance.

But if people knew *how* Leningrad is suffering!

And we still have a long winter ahead of us. The frosts are grim. Today it is warmer, but then there is a snowstorm instead. Outside the city I'm sure there is a blizzard.

One cannot listen unmoved to the people of this dark, hungry, frozen city rejoicing in the frosts because the Germans are dying from the same cold at the Front.

'Serves them right!' people repeat. This from lips blue with cold as they stand inside the covered gateways during the shelling.

The Leningrad blockade is usually called the 'Fire Ring' ... No, an ice ring would be more appropriate.

I have just started on the second part of my poem. In it I shall try to describe one Leningrad night.

5th January, 1942

Artillery shelling of our district—even of our grounds. Shells were bursting so close that the chiefs proposed that we should leave the front rooms of the main building.

A few days ago I had a dream. It was that I, and some people who were invisible in the darkness, stood in the covered gateway, waiting for the bombardment to end. Hollow, luminous spheres rushed by. 'Take care of spray, they are mustard-gas spinning tops!' someone was shouting. I woke with a constricted heart.

People are saying that we have occupied Mga. But who heard this news? And how? After all, hardly any radios work.

6th January, 1942

Today I revisited Casualty for the first time. I went through two bathrooms; the baths were filled with clean water, but no one was taking a bath.

In the first room a completely naked male corpse lay on a stretcher. A skeleton would have been fatter. Here was something that didn't even look as if it had been a live body, with flesh and blood and muscles. On the abdomen, in a hollow, a note was pinned with the name of the deceased. I didn't read it.

The eyes of the dead man were open, and on his face there was growing a 'cadaver' beard, which is proof against any razor. The nose stuck out in a frightening manner.

In the next room several stretchers were placed in a row. Bodies of men and women were on these. A quite inhuman thinness deprived them of age, or even sex.

I was surprised to see that the first body had a little blood on its leg, just below the knee. He must have fallen or been knocked down by someone. I thought, How was this? There must have been blood in this body, so there must have been life in it.

In the other rooms, in the corridors, patients sit or lie as a matter of course. They are on benches, on stretchers, or simply on the floor. The sole difference here is that they are wearing clothes. Only their eyes are alive. They stay for hours at a stretch. Two women doctors move amongst them. They look like corpses themselves.

No one is being treated here, only fed. There is only one illness—starvation. A workman is lying on one of the benches. Alive. He moves his lips and repeats one sentence. 'Seventeen years . . . seventeen years on the production line.'

On another bench an old woman, or perhaps she isn't old—half dead; only her eyes are alive. Her lips are purple. Next to her a crutch or a stick, and an empty bag. Probably straight from the queue.

And in the midst of all this horror there are a few who feign, pretend they are starving, but who are not mortally ill. They will make their way across the whole city for a bowl of soup . . . and they will fight over a morsel of food from those . . . in the bathroom.

Shall we have enough strength to wait for the blockade to lift? And how many will be alive to rejoice that they live?

7th January, 1942

Yesterday the city telephones ceased to function all over the building. I don't know the situation in other important buildings—apparently it is the same everywhere. At first homes were cut off, now it is the turn of institutes. But the city is holding out. It has got to.

I attended a lecture by Professor Tushinky on 'The Illness of Starvation'. That is its actual title.

The body consists of fat and muscle. Our layers of fat are our fur coat as it were, and the muscles manufacture warmth. When the fur coat disappears, and when the 'factory' ceases to work, we die. By then we have consumed our muscles, our 'emergency reserve'. The decrease of weight goes unevenly. The temperature is evenly reduced during the course of the day.

The liver represents the food store—a normal liver weighs 1,500 grammes, that of a starving person 700.

The outward manifestation of starvation is seen in swelling, and at times by drying up. Those who suffer from swelling have their blood diluted, and also the blood itself swells.

The skin is dry, deprived of sweat and fat; the specific facial expression is apathy.

Glucose resuscitates strength miraculously, whether it is given intravenously or by mouth. This is why ballet dancers eat up to fifty grammes of glucose after a long solo appearance.

With starving people one notices the need for carbo-hydrates—that is for bread. After all, Professor Pavlov has said, 'Our organism is very wise. It wants what is good for it.'

Amongst other things of interest to me, I learned why we haven't had a typhus epidemic . . . it seems it is because of the Blockade. New viruses do not reach us, and the strain we already have has become weak and feeble. Thus the same blockade which is starving the city to death is saving it from infection.

And people still say that General Meretzkov's units will be in Leningrad by January 10th . . . well, if not the 10th but the 15th, 20th, by the end of the month. So long as they are there!

They can't have been in history, nor can there be in the future, a more shattering event as the meeting of the people of the city and the army!

And our main difficulties—no radio, no papers, now—no telephone. Nobody knows anything. And nothing from my family. Not a word. Apparently the telephone line has had another direct hit. Are they alive? Are they well? Did they receive the money I sent?

On the 27th January, Mishenka will be a year old. Let the Blockade be lifted by that day, if not sooner!

Quarter to seven. Evening

Shelling. At first it seemed to me that logs of wood were falling fast—log after log. And later I thought, But where have all those logs come from? And all at once it became clear . . . shelling.

8th January, 1942. About 11 a.m.

Yesterday was a difficult day. During the morning the light went off. There was no current until this morning. We ate only in the morning (substitute coffee, substitute milk, but how delicious it tasted!). I have eaten a little porridge but—(a shell somewhere near) and . . . I'm going down to the shelter. The shelling is getting worse.

Half past twelve

Came back. The shelling is over. The barrage wasn't a long one. Rather like the one we had the other day at the Sitnoy Market.

My article went to Kuibyshev to the Soviet Information Bureau, and from there to America. Today is the last date for the advance sent to me by Afinogenov. Now, if I receive confirmation that the article has arrived and is suitable, I shall write regularly, three times monthly.

I began to make preparations for sending the article a few days ago. First, I re-transcribed it according to the rules of the Exchange Telegraph: 'Am sending first article under the title quote that is how we live unquote fullstop new para two Leningrad fronts exist colon a battle front and a way of life fullstop the first dash at the approaches to the city where the Red Army is fighting the second dash the city itself fullstop', and so on.

Yesterday I darned yet again I.D.'s woollen socks and mittens. I washed the scarf in the hope of making it warmer by making it fluffier. The frosts are grim. Yesterday I left bread for I.D. After all, he was facing a journey on foot across the whole city, to the main post office. This is the only one that accepts telegraph messages, and that only when the electricity is working. Just in case, I gave him a candle for the telegraph girl.

I.D. got up at dawn and went on his errand. He has only just returned. The hardest thing is the lack of electricity, so that one cannot work in the evenings. And the evenings start soon after four in the afternoon. It is fairly dark in the daytime, although the days are frosty and clear. And that's how it is at present.

Yesterday evening, in order to anticipate today's march to the telegraph office, I thought up a festive supper. We used the little paraffin lamp (the last of the paraffin) and I laid on a sumptuous meal. Half a small onion—the second half will be eaten today—cut into small pieces, thickly salted and dressed with sunflower oil. All this with bread—three slices each. The crumbs we put in a plate, soaked in the remains of the oil, and divided equally. In addition, we drank the remains of the wine: port Ararat, highest grade. After this feast we went to bed, feeling extraordinarily happy. Our Princess Myshkina appeared (so she is still alive) in the darkness. She scurried along the table picking up crumbs like a bird. Then she fell into the (naturally) empty milk jug. We lit a match, and the Princess, making a last effort, scrambled from the milk jug—what an effort that was—and disappeared.

We shall have no light. Current will be switched on for three to four hours out of the twenty-four, but at unstated times, maybe at night.

9th January, 1942. About 2 p.m.

Intense artillery shelling. I.D. is next door, He is examining students . . . I am calm.

Jeanne, my little girl. I try not to think about her. But it is no use. Her letters frighten me more than the heaviest shelling. How restless she is, poor darling. She sent the child to a crèche, as she thought it would be better for him, now she wants to take him back as he caught chicken-pox there, only mildly, according to her. But it can't take much to kill such a tiny creature.

Jeanne writes: 'His little face is so pretty. One can see he is no longer a baby, that soon he'll be a year old. But his little body is so thin, and he hasn't any teeth. One's heart is torn to pieces . . . all the little vests and jerseys made when he was born still fit him, they have become short, but they are still right otherwise.'

And I read this, and I think: I remember how he lay there in his tiny cap . . . why did I let them take him away? But what good could I have done?

I.D. comforts me. I myself have the feeling that things will get better when this winter is over.

Everyone notices that I.D. has got much thinner. I try to give him my share of the ration—after all, I need less food. But, of course, it isn't enough for him.

Molotov's note to our allies about the German atrocities in the occupied areas has appeared. I haven't read it yet, and, of course, the radio is silent. Just now it produced some sort of a sound—it turned out to be testing the local radio-relay centre. The shelling has stopped.

13th January, 1942

It's getting dark. I have no light, but I must write down immediately what I have heard, with my own ears. The whistle of a railway engine. One weak whistle, but clear and distinctive. The first whistle during the whole time of the Blockade.

We all ran out into the courtyard to check if it were true. Silence. Frost. Everything covered with snow. We stand there and listen. Dr Pozharskaya stands beside me. She reminds me of my late mother, not so much by her features as by the look of her face. We listened together, and then we looked at each other, yes; they were railway-train whistles.

We had been told about the ice track across Lake Ladoga. So it is true, it has begun to work! And later on trains will carry food supplies from Ladoga to the city. It is our lifeline, perhaps our salvation.

14th January, 1942. 4 p.m.

A ferocious frost. I am sitting in my overcoat and gloves and reading Timiryazev. I know his name, respect and venerate him as a scientist of world-wide repute, brilliant at popularising his subject. But, in fact, I know nothing about him. To tell the truth, he is for me a rather unsuccessful statue at the Nikitsky Gate, a narrow, dark figure, with sides as if sliced off, in a long cloak. The hands, hidden underneath, are folded formally, like a schoolboy at a *viva voce* . . . This monument was knocked down during the first raids on Moscow, and while I was still there. But in a few days Timiryazev was back again as if nothing had happened, standing in his old place, with his hands folded. He was put back very quickly.

I read through Timiryazev's book about chlorophyll, the green substance of plants.

'The life of a plant', writes Timiryazev, 'is a constant transformation of the energy of the sun's rays into a chemical tension—life of an animal—the transformation of chemical tension into heat and movement.' He goes on to say that it is as if a coiled spring is wound up on the sun, which descends to earth. And this uncoiled spring is just life.

'A grain of chlorophyll is a link connecting a magnificent explosion of energy in our central luminary Body with all the manifold expressions of life on the planet inhabited by us.'

Timiryazev quotes Bolzmann and Newton. Newton wrote: 'Apparently nature likes transformations', and further: 'In the series of such varied and strange transformations why shouldn't nature turn bodies into light and light into bodies?' Newton had only been guessing at what Timiryazev knew.

Bolzmann wrote: 'The plants unfold the unmeasurable

surface of their leaves and force the Solar energy before it falls to the level of the Earth's temperature to prompt chemical synthesis, not yet investigated and not yet known to our laboratories.'

'Unmeasurable surface of leaves' . . . these words evoke in me a swaying ocean of green foliage and light particles flying towards us through the icy space of the universe.

15th January, 1942. 9.15 in the evening

Last night the mortuary was on fire. Half-burnt bodies from a factory—also on fire—had been brought there (these fires are really quite calamitous now). The bodies were in quilted jackets which were still smouldering, but nobody noticed this. The fire which lurked between the layers of cotton wool gradually worked its way out. The flames bursting from the jackets enveloped the old dry boxes, brought in for making coffins. Everything was filled with smoke.

The head of the Fire Defence came running and began to pull the bodies apart with his hands. The fire had to be buried under snow, but the mortuary was saved.

As soon as this fire was over, another broke out, on the opposite side of the Karpovka, along the fence of the Botanical Gardens, where a number of army lorries were parked.

A petrol tank had caught fire from a carelessly lit bonfire. Then another caught, and another. Then the tractor of a third. This was uncoupled from the petrol tank at risk of life. The second lorry was out of control and was pushed into the Karpovka, where it fell, crashing through the ice. The resultant pillar of fire shot up and was higher than our boiler-room chimney—and that is forty metres high.

During all this time I have been very busy. The day is so short and there is no light. Although there are practically no household chores, it is necessary to do some sewing and darning every day. My mania for tidiness is costing me a great deal of energy. On the other hand, it is particularly important to keep everything clean.

Still, I have managed to do quite a lot. Yesterday I wrote seven stanzas (7 × 6 = 42) and that is a lot for me. That is why I haven't written about A.

A. is a fellow Muscovite. At present he is writing (as far as I can gather) a philosophical treatise called 'The Spirit of

War'. In connection with this he decided he ought to cast an eye on Leningrad. Besides, there are relations of his wife here, and naturally they are starving.

I do not know which of these two reasons is the most important, but whichever it is, A. achieved the almost impossible and arrived here on an army plane which was bringing decorations and paper money.

Having got my address from Ketlinskaya, A. appeared at our place in the evening. I was called on the internal telephone and told: 'A writer from Moscow wishes to see you.'

A writer from Moscow, oh God! I wrapped my head in a scarf and ran down into the icy darkness.

In the light of a small paraffin lamp I saw A. His face was familiar, but as often happens to me I couldn't put a name to it. But though he was practically a stranger, how precious he was to me! He was someone from the world *outside*. I embraced him; I was out of my mind with joy. I made him comfortable on the sofa.

'Talk to me, tell me about everything,' I said, over and over again. He looked at me with tenderness and compassion. I must have looked very different.

In the course of conversation he told me, as if I already knew it, about the death of Afinogenov, in Moscow.

'It can't be!' I cried, remembering Afinogenov's eyes, his jaunty dimple, the light-hearted way he went through life. He was successful in everything, and now he was lost . . . it's not true, it can't be true . . . and then I bowed to the inevitable. No, it was true. It is so.

A. came next day. We walked with him in the hospital yard. He looked at our buildings, at the frozen trees, at people's faces. He couldn't speak. He was stunned.

And now already he has flown back to Moscow.

17th January, 1942

A short but fairly intensive shelling half an hour ago. When it was over, I.D. went to the main post office to send money to his relations and to Jeanne. District post offices do not function, there being no light and, of course, no heat. And in one of them, which rumour said had one candle, no member of the staff turned up; all were either ill or dead. Because of the lack of light, the bank is closed too. On account of this, I am unable to get money from the broadcasting administration. People say that payment will be made in the last quarter of January.

Good news from the Front! I was told at the radio offices that Fedyuninsky has begun a general offensive, and that fighting is going on in the Lake Ilmen district. The Germans are reporting on it. They say that the scale of the fighting is bigger than the Moscow one. But these—which may be the last trials of Leningrad—are the heaviest yet.

And frosts on top of everything . . .

Lelya P., for whom we found a job as housekeeper in the military hospital, is ill with pneumonia, and is now a patient here. I went to visit her.

20th January, 1942. Morning

I was so busy with my poem and with the housework that there simply hasn't been time to write daily in my diary, which is what I would want to do.

During the past few days I have corrected and revised the first part. Now passages which seemed powerful to me at the time have had to be moved to another place because they are weakened by new stanzas. I have rewritten the passages on humanism. Never have I worked with such passion. Even at night, lying down, I cannot stop. I am dying of tiredness and still my brain goes on, and everything is vital. And I find a place for everything I want to say, like in an already-prepared nest. This is the first sign that consciousness is fully given to the work, and assimilates everything.

On Sunday (again under shelling) we went to Pesochnaya. Our flat is terrible—an icy chaos. Temperature minus five.

Marfusha, Lelya's cleaner (dependant's ration card), died on the 13th. In the dining room there were dirty beds, litter, empty bottles of vegetable oil, a paraffin lamp, an axe, firewood—and on everything a layer of greasy soot. On the soot-covered walls the plates still hang—the porcelain, the faïence.

In the third room, where the glass had been blown out from the bombing some time ago, there were also bundles of dirty, icy sheets. The bath was filled with ice.

The Students' Hostel has been transferred to the lower floors where it is warmer.

At night Dina Osipovna and Inna go out on to the landing and sit there, huddled against the warm radiator. Here, according to them, they reach a state of euphoria and dream of the future.

As usual, there is nothing from Jeanne. Her last letter, sent as long ago as November, was anxious. The boy is mortally ill. Jeanne wrote: 'Yura and I didn't undress at all. We took it in turns to give Misha oxygen. He opened his little mouth like a fledgling when the tube was brought to him. In general he behaves magnificently (if one can say such a thing about a ten-month baby). He endures the hardest suction cups and mustard plasters and takes his medicine.'

My only consolation is that this letter was followed by another which said Mishenka is improving.

Today there are twenty-eight degrees of frost.

20th January, 1942. Evening

'Meridian' is getting on splendidly. Even at night it refuses to let me sleep, it insists that I go on writing.

If only I had sufficient health and strength! . . .

21st January, 1942

Important news. The bread ration is increased. Manual workers get an additional fifty grammes, white-collar workers a hundred grammes.

Great success at the Kalinin front. We have taken Kholm.

Grim, severe frosts here, almost thirty-five degrees.

25th January, 1942

It appears that there were forty degrees of frost yesterday, and apparently no less today. The day after tomorrow, Mishenka will be a year old. His first rattle (a tiny celluloid drum with a pea inside) hangs by a ribbon at the head of my bed.

Read to patients in our eye clinic.

Seven o'clock in the evening

Our position is catastrophic. Just now a crowd destroyed the wooden fence of the hospital grounds, and carried it away for firewood.

There is no water, and if the bakery stops even for a single day what happens? We have no soup, only porridge. In the morning there was coffee, but there won't be any more to drink.

As to water—we have half the kettle (we are keeping it in hot sand), half a saucepan for washing, and a quarter of a carafe for tomorrow. That is *all*.

26th January, 1942

For the first time I cried from grief and fury: inadvertently I overturned the saucepan of porridge on the stove. I.D. nevertheless swallowed a few spoonfuls, mixed with the ashes.

There is still no bread. But to make up I wrote three very good stanzas and the end piece of the chapter 'Light and Warmth'.

I am able to write as never before. But at nights I sleep badly: my fingers are growing numb all the time. At first small needles, then larger, larger, less and less frequent. And, finally, a complete numbness. My hands atrophy.

27th January, 1942

The bakery did not stop work, after all, as we were afraid it would. When the water mains packed up, eight thousand Young Communist League members—weakened like everyone else from starvation—chilled to the bone, formed a chain from the Neva to the bakery tables, and passed to them the water from hand to hand.

Yesterday there were enormous queues at the bakers' shops. Bread wasn't delivered till the evening, but still it was there.

Today, at the very hour of midnight, Mishenka will be a year old.

29th January, 1942

'Household' chores are taking up more and more time. The stove, the kettle, washing up, warming up soup or porridge, darning, washing smalls, take up half the day.

Today I carried out a spring clean, of which I had been dreaming for some time. Most of our clothing I put together neatly in a large suitcase to await better days—perhaps when there is water and light, perhaps when the Blockade is lifted. I prevailed upon Efrosiniya Ivanovna to wash a second lot of things that we need with the famous water from the small river Karpovka which alone provides our washing and drinking water. We have strained it through eight layers of gauze, but even so the water is dreadful.

I put my smart dresses into the bottom of the suitcase. Our rubber overshoes are beginning to crack, so I have stuffed them tightly with paper, and wrapped them in up old rags—like putting away our camp equipment for the winter. I have put away my typewriter also, the ribbon is getting very dry from the cold. I removed the electric lamp from the table, as it is completely superfluous.

Now everything is in perfect order, but I haven't worked for two days.

We have our difficulties with bread. It is brought in small consignments, straight from the bakery, damp and crushed. There are long queues.

30th January, 1942

During the last few days it's not only faces that have changed. The look of the city has changed as well. All the fences, amongst them ours, have disappeared. But the beautiful centuries-old birch and lime trees have been left alone.

Some kind of a new topography has established itself. Crossing side streets, lanes, short cuts, connecting courtyards to go through.

Today the funeral took place of Professor A. A. Likhachev. The body, without a coffin (this arrived later), was lying in the Conference Hall, on an oval table, placed on a piece of plywood.

The body was in a sheet. Around the table, in the icy room, stood the professors and assistant lecturers. I.D. made a speech. I watched him. He took off his fur hat but kept on a black silk cap because of the cold. And he himself is thin and yellow. But his speech was in good, traditional style, with the Latin Sursum Corda (Let us lift our spirit) at the end.

31st January, 1942

Pipes laid underground have burst, because the water inside is frozen and therefore still. It is not engine-driven. When the water is moving, it is as if it were saving itself by fleeing from the frost. When it doesn't move, the frost catches up with it and when it freezes it bursts the pipes.

2nd February, 1942

I crave to write as one sometimes craves to eat. As a matter of fact, I work at night instead of sleeping. As soon as I lie down, it is as if my brain says: 'Now our hour has arrived; let us start!' So we start.

My sleep is so shallow, so light, that I am half awake, and at once in my consciousness I find a line, even a stanza. The lines are standing at the door, waiting to be let in, and as soon as the smallest chink appears, they are in.

Natasha saw two bodies locked in an embrace at the entrance to one of our clinics.

By now it is known for certain that Lapin and Khatsrevin have perished in Kiev.

8th February, 1942. In the evening

I have never felt so low as I do now. Two little oil lamps will be the death of me. I crave for light as one craves for bread or even for air. On top of everything, I spilt the soup again, this time when I was taking it out of the oven. I had to clean up the greasy mess on the floor. (Thank goodness the floor is stone.)

My heart is so heavy that I can hardly write, but even today I managed to do some work.

Lelya put it very well when she said that if only she could stroke a dog or a cat—a pet animal, as she said—or at least if she could hear barking or mewing, she would feel better.

The quiet at times drives me nearly out of my mind—now, for instance; there isn't a sound, or even a rustle.

In the next room Sofia Vasilyevna, I.D.'s laboratory assistant, sleeps in her fur coat. In all probability she has neither undressed herself nor washed for three months. She is on the verge of madness, terrified of losing her ration cards, and with cause, as she has now lost them for three months in succession. I don't even know what she exists on. This indeed is death by starvation.

I write and write . . . if only our people would come back from the District Committee—if only there was some life in the dark, icy corridors.

In my mind's eye I constantly see a mother and daughter who might have stepped out of the pages of Dostoievsky. The mother—an old-age pensioner; her daughter Lyulya, sixteen years old, who is living with her. The child wears an old-fashioned hood and carries a little muff. She has wide, astonished eyes. Some dishonest woman tracked them down in a queue, got to know them, wormed her way into their confidence, began to call on them at home, and finally promised to get Lyulya a job as a dish-washer in the 21st Military Hospital. She brought along a written agreement to take the girl on the staff. (All false.) It is not even known that such a hospital exists. At the beginning of the month, when new ration cards are issued, this Lady Bountiful arrived to fetch the mother and daughter. At eight in the evening, in complete darkness, she led them into our main building. (Evidently she herself works here as an orderly or something.) She took both ration cards from the girl, her own and her mother's, for the entire month, also forty-five roubles in cash which the mother had borowed. All this was allegedly to buy food . . . and instead she vanished into the darkness.

The girl heard her voice. 'I am here, follow me . . .' Exactly as in the *Ratcatcher* by Green. And that was all.

It is impossible to forget the mother and her daughter. The mother repeated in a heart-rending voice, again and again, 'Lyulya, what have you done to me! You have put me alive into my grave!' Whereas Lyulya, pressing her little muff convulsively to her breast, whispered, 'What is in store for tonight?' Evidently afraid her mother will finish her off with her tears.

We started at once to write a declaration for the Militia. But what use is such a declaration today? And what can the Militia do?

So we do not know what has become of them.

5th February, 1942

All our staff has gone to the Smolny. Once again there are new plans concerning the evacuation. Thus, we too might move. Where to? To Irkutsk, it seems.

9th February, 1942

There is so much I have to do. But as if to spite me, the urge to write is irresistible. I attended a conference of Baltic writers. I received an invitation through Vishnevsky. The conference was to take place on Vasiliyevsky Island, a long way from us, and to last for two days. It was a major expedition, staying away for a night.

I discussed it with I.D. and we decided I must go. So once again I began a great orgy of darning stockings and mittens, and I also organised my food. In the kitchen I was given in exchange for two dinners and two lunches, a couple of eggs, nearly new, and a small piece of old cheese. I.D., in his turn, gave me a quarter of a bar of chocolate from our emergency reserve. Thus I was richly equipped.

We had to start at ten in the morning, as punctually as if we were on board ship. On the day we got up at six in the morning. The walk alone would take two hours, and we walk slowly now.

The morning was uncommonly beautiful. The more severe the frost, the more tender are the colours of the dawn sky, as everyone knows.

We left the house at sunrise. On the Bolshoi Prospekt, where the trams were deeply buried under snow, was a house that had been on fire, the flames were dying down. This fire had apparently been fought all night. Most surprisingly, there was water. It was still flowing from the fire hydrant and flooding the whole street. It made a large lake, reflected pink from the dawn light, while mist drifted over it.

Lost in contemplation of the sun, I fell as far as my knees in the mess of water, snow and ice. I felt as if I was in icy boots, holding my leg in a vice. And thus I walked the whole way. Only when the conference was under way did strips of ice begin to fall off my boots . . . Towards the end of the first day, after the report and the speech, I was asked to read some of my work. I read 'Light and Warmth', the second chapter which isn't finished yet.

Ketlinskaya and I, as women and guests, spent the night comfortably on bunks behind curtains, in the room where the conference took place. The room was opaque from cigarette and tobacco smoke, but on the credit side it had been warmed up by human breath and a small but very zealous little stove.

Towards the morning, I woke up with cold and I realised that the stove had gone out. But immediately I heard a crackling sound (the sort of sound you get when a water melon is cut open). It was Z., who was demolishing with an axe the chair on which he had sat during the conference. I watched him throw the pieces into the stove—hapless Leningrad chairs! I grew warm again and fell asleep.

The individual speeches by the Baltic writers were interesting. Some remarks, especially, hit the nail on the head. I shall write some of them down.

'Exits', 'fly-outs' and 'crawl-outs' to the advanced front line . . . the latter, about the crawlers.

'The poetry of the exact execution of the military manual.'

'Galloping situation.'

'The ships broke through, mainly on the basis of the political moral state of the people, because the boilers weren't working any more.'

'A peaceful dug-out situation.'

'Led out the men without losses, with the exception of himself.'

'A submarine loves depth. Close to the shore it cannot exist.'

'Trawlers—ploughmen of the sea.'

'A submarine does not like white nights.'

Our propaganda leaflets were sent over the front like by bows and arrows. Two people stretched the bow string and a third one released the arrow which was covered in leaflets.

At the end of the second day I was taken home by car.

12th February, 1942

I.D. worries me. He looks very ill; he has lost a lot of weight and feels cold all the time. He walks slowly, leaning on his stick. Worst of all is the state of his hands—the joints are red and swollen, the skin is stretched tight and looks like leather.

The second part moves on slowly, but, as before, it is going well.

Nothing from Jeanne. But I console myself by thinking that there is probably a letter lying in the great mass of unsorted mail in our local post office, and that it is impossible to find it. Other people, however, get letters. . . .

16th February, 1942

Yesterday, as we agreed, I went to the destroyer, to give a talk. In order to reach the destroyer, we had a two hours' walk as it is at the other end of the town. I walked along slowly, preserving my strength. But in the middle of the Kirov Bridge, where the rise begins, I suddenly felt as if I might fall down at any moment. . . . My legs were like cotton wool and refused to hold me. I realised I hadn't got the strength to reach my goal, and I just managed to reach Ketlinskaya to warn her and Zonin that I couldn't make it. They went without me, and I crawled along to the Ozerskys' to rest.

I had some food and a rest. Then they put me in an armchair near the stove and they all sat near me: Nikolai Ivanovich, Alena and Kovrov. To the accompaniment of intense shelling (the day before a shell hit a nearby window, nearly killing Alena) I read both parts—one after the other. Everyone was very excited.

And now I am interested in this question—will everyone be affected in the way we are, or only the people who have been through the Leningrad Blockade?

17th February, 1942

Once again (seriously, this time) there is talk about evacuating the Institute. Even a date is planned, the 15th March. And the place—Arkhangelsk (Archangel). And Leningrad . . . how can we leave it? Six years have been spent here, if one counts a month for a year, as was done during the defence of Sebastopol in the Crimean War, not this one. No, it must be counted more here.

If we go, we shall take Lelya and Inna with us. Dina Osipovna is dying.

18th February, 1942

Yesterday I gave a talk at the hospital where T. is lying. He is worse. Tomorrow I give a talk in the hospital attached to the Herzen Institute. Then after tomorrow at the meeting of active party members. On the 21st I am going with a delegation from our district to the front line . . . so I am going, after all! The only thing I am afraid of is of freezing to death.

19th February, 1942

I have just received a letter from the children, written in December. Our Mishenka is dead. He didn't reach his first birthday.

20th February, 1942

I read yesterday's letter from the children, devouring every word. And all of a sudden I hit the following lines, while reading at top speed.

'We cannot reconcile ourselves to this great grief—Mishenka's death. Our life in Chistopol now seems to us completely empty and pointless. After all, the reason for our being here has gone. . . . All at once it is very quiet in our tiny room. Perhaps when the thaw starts we shall be able to get a boat back to Moscow.'

I read this letter to the end. Then I put it aside . . . then very quickly I took it and read it again, vaguely hopeful that I had imagined. No, it is all true.

21st February, 1942

Tomorrow I am going to the Front with a delegation from our District Committee. It is good that I am going. It will help me to bear the pain which the heart finds it difficult to master.

23rd February, 1942

The Red Army Day. Gorokhovetz. Snow, snow, everywhere! I am writing in Gorokhovetz, in the Political Department of General Fedyuninsky's army. It is a log house that must have belonged to well-to-do people in the past. Photographs on the walls, pot-pourri on the chest of drawers, but in the entrance hall saddles, canvas bags, rifles, felt boots, skis, petrol cans.

Over the little house, in the vast frosty sky, the weak drone of an engine, and the shining speck of a plane. It was explained to me that this was 'Adolf' flying. The sound of anti-aircraft guns is different here out in the open; not like in Leningrad where it echoes off the tall houses.

Yesterday—was it only yesterday?—I.D. led me once more before dawn to our Petrograd District Committee in Skoro-khodov Street, where the delegates were to meet. We went through several communicating courtyards. The stars were still shining. The house of the District Committee was echoing and empty. The lights were on (it is only at the District Committees that there is still electricity). A kettle was boiling.

Soon, we, the delegates, were all assembled. We were put in a small lorry protected at the sides by plywood screens. The starry sky made the fourth side—the back. During our journey the stars gradually paled, only shining Venus accompanied us for a long time, until dawn extinguished it.

Only when we were leaving did we learn where we were actually going. It turned out to be on the other side of Lake Ladoga, behind the ring of the Blockade, two hundred kilometres from Leningrad. I.D. was rather upset, but waved cheerfully in farewell.

In the lorry the seats were narrow, uncomfortable benches with nothing to lean back against. The smell of bad petrol choked us. Next to me there was a great can of the stuff, as tall as I am. It was splashing over and still we lacked fuel.

We were stationary for a fairly long time in the Smolny District, waiting for delegations from other districts. Finally everyone turned up.

We were carrying presents to the Front. Five automatic rifles with an inscription on the stock: 'To the best exterminators of German occupants', camouflage gowns, shaving tackle, tobacco, leather and fur gloves, bags for commanding officers, handkerchiefs, guitars and mandolins. I didn't think any of these would arrive intact, they were badly packed and fell over on their sides when the road was bumpy. They cried and moaned as if they were alive. We supported them with our arms and backs.

For Fedyuninsky himself we took a small leather box for tobacco. There were different gifts from different districts, but the 'order of the day' was the same from everyone—to break through the ring of the Blockade.

The journey lasted thirteen hours. It was cold and exhausting, but not beyond endurance.

We crossed Lake Ladoga in an hour and a half. The ice is still firm, but the driver told us that at noon, when the sun is strong, they won't allow five-ton lorries to cross any more. After all, the ice is riddled with bomb craters. After the rough, bumpy snow road, the ice of the lake seemed like bliss to me. It neither rocked nor shook.

Having crossed the lake, we circled for a long time round a place, begging for petrol. For the first time I saw a live goat, a live dog and a live chicken. People looked out from all the other lorries, eying this miracle. Beyond the Lake we heard singing for the first time. I looked at my fellow travellers; they were all stunned.

Altogether the difference between us and the people here is astonishing. Here the people have rosy cheeks, they talk fast, they take deep breaths, and thick clouds of steam come out of of their mouths. We are pale and our breath is shallow. (An almost invisible cloud comes out of our mouths.) We walk slowly and talk quietly.

We saw a threatening fire at Zhikharevo. A tank with

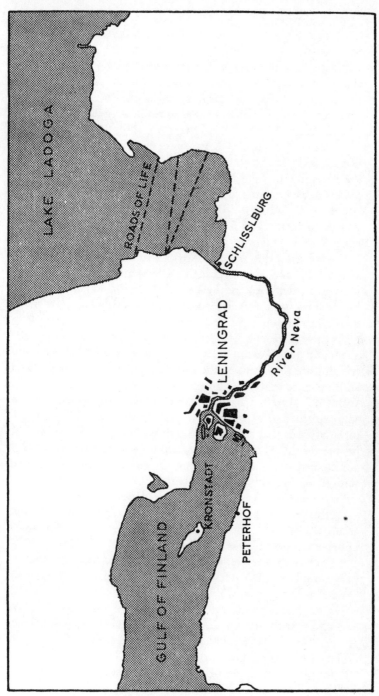

The 'Roads of Life' across Lake Ladoga

'Tavot', a tanker carrying paraffin, and railway trucks laden with peat had just been set on fire by the Germans on the narrow-gauge railway, and were burning on the line. Everything—just as it was brought up. The Germans flew over it in the morning, spied their targets, and at sundown bombed them with such precision that the engine could not get near enough to pull the train.

Never in my life did I see such flames, purple, thick as a feather-bed with black smoke twisted round, it seemed to heave itself heavily into the air.

Before we had time to regain our senses, the bombing started. Bombs fell quite close. But more frightening than the bombs was the machine-gun fire with which the Germans raked each car and lorry. Our anti-aircraft guns were obviously inadequate.

Everyone lay down in the snow, including the soldiers. Some people left our lorry and some remained inside it. Sychev, from the works, two men and I sat inside the plywood covers of the lorry (crass stupidity) and only winced and lowered our necks when the shrapnel whistled over us.

At this moment I thought with passionate tenderness of our shelter in Leo Tolstoi Street, and those merciful stone walls which bore the brunt of the blows. But here—just sky and air and bursts of machine-gun fire.

But our stupidity had a grain of sense—a strategic ruse! It was explained to us that the only reason the Germans didn't hit our lorry was that it couldn't occur to them that there could be people inside. They thought it was an abandoned machine.

Fifteen to twenty planes flew in circles over the ill-fated station. After a tiny breather there was another shout:

'The second run is beginning. Lie down!'

At this point even I crawled out of the lorry, and just as I was about to lie down in a ditch, a soldier rose up from it. I understood that all was over.

Of our group, the boldest-looking girl was the most shamefully afraid of all of us. (Strong anti-aircraft fire. Evidently 'Adolf' is quite near us.)

We are about to drive to X Division, to visit the gunners. We carry with us the issue of the Division's newspaper, *Into the Decisive Battle,* which has just appeared, and in which Stalin's order is printed.

I am glad to be here. My heart is less heavy. It's a pity that we didn't succeed in seeing General Fedyuninsky. Yesterday evening he went into one of the little houses at his H.Q., but not the one where we spent the night. Lucky were those who were spending the night in that other house; they all got up and Fedyuninsky chatted with them for a long time.

He was very gay and came in after having his banya (sauna). He said it was excellent, but that the steam bath was a bit cold. The General likes warmth. How well I sympathise with him!

The guns have started growling. The house shudders. The cars drive up. We move off.

24th February, 1942. X Division. Morning

Woke up during the night. Where was I? Then it came to me— in a dugout. We are on plank beds, covered with branches of fir. Varya Nikolayevna Volk from the District Committee is next to me. Then comes Sychev, then the others. The man on duty tosses some more small logs on the stove—resinous smoke stings the eyes. Suddenly a gun thunders. I don't know whose, but here at advanced border positions all this seems less frightening than it does in Leningrad.

In the early morning a man brought us plates of porridge, bread and for each a large slice of butter. What a marvellous thing! Next time I shall bring a spoon with me without fail.

26th February, 1942. Leningrad

I am back home, lying on my bed, and still I cannot get warm. I have an eiderdown over me, a rug and a coat over my legs. I am in my warm dressing gown, and the room temperature is fourteen degrees. Almost every hour I am given a hot drink, yet I do not feel any warmer.

During the journey to the Front I wasn't wearing anything really warm. It is true someone found some trousers lined with cotton wool for me, and a jacket to wear under my coat. But this was old stuff that had been disinfected often. The cotton wool was nearly worn out. On my head I wore my invariable woollen bonnet. I had a muff for my hands, a plaid and white knitted scarf. I borrowed this last from Klavdiya Ivanovna, on oath that I would take care of it as I would of a bread ration card.

I reminded myself of Korobochka in Gogol's *Dead Souls* more than anything else.

But all this was bearable. That I.D., an experienced worrier, a participant in two wars, a doctor and a thoughtful husband should fail to give me anything containing spirits was a triple mistake.

He should have seen me on the way back, after we had crossed the Lake. I was drinking spirits, together with fat and sugar, with the drivers. It seems to me that it's only thanks to this that I'm still alive.

There was a moment when the driver (I was put into his cab out of pity) looked closely at me and said:

'Well now, all you have to do is to pray to God that I don't have any trouble with the lorry. If I have to stop the engine, it will put paid to you.'

And it's true—only the engine kept me warm.

Lake Ladoga is an enormous plain of ice and snow—as on the Pole. Everything is made of snow—fences, made solid or with snow bricks, semicircular igloos for the anti-aircraft crews, foundations for the anti-aircraft guns. Everything is virgin clean, white almost blue, and over it all the gentle vault of blue sky. Everything that is not white comes as a shock to the eye. The poppy-red flag of the traffic scout can be seen from a kilometre away. Not for nothing it is said here, 'Snow is the life-line for the soldier. He digs himself into it, drinks it, washes himself in it.'

My long sight, which is a nuisance when I am reading or writing, is most useful here. I could see nearly everything, right up to the horizon. There, on the frozen lake road, multi-coloured dots are moving . . . there are the lorries. If they are pink, it means mutton carcasses are being transported, if black—coal, if yellow—boxes made of bark with I don't know what in them, smooth and white, almost indistinguishable from the snow—bags of flour. This is our daily bread, our life-line, sent to Leningrad from the Great Earth.*

The labour of the Ladoga lorry drivers is a sacred labour.

It is enough to cast an eye on the road. This worn-out, bombed, tormented road which knows no peace, day or night. Its snow is turned to sand. Wrecked machines and spare parts are lying everywhere—in ruts, pot-holes, ditches, in bomb craters, there are wrecked vehicles.

* Landmass in Soviet hands as distinguished from enclaves within German occupation held by the partisans or besieged places.

And this is the road that the Ladoga drivers cross four times a day under bombing and shell-fire. It is for them that everywhere there are notices printed in scarlet on shields: 'DRIVER HAVE YOU DONE TWO RUNS TODAY?' And indeed each driver does his two trips.

We reached Gorokhovetz, the Army H.Q., late in the evening. The moon was bright, surrounded by a frosty, hazy circle. All indications are there was an even more severe frost on the moon than ours down on earth.

As soon as our cars arrived at H.Q. they were speedily removed to the fir grove and hidden there. We were told that because of the full moon we were travelling in a dangerous zone. But it was quiet—so much quieter than on the Nevsky, in Leningrad.

We left Gorokhovetz for Leningrad during the night, while the stars were still out. Gradually, the enemy rockets grew paler and paler. Dawn came up over the forest, a pale green sky like an apple which turned red on one side. And that was the moment the driver told me to pray for the engine, otherwise I should freeze to death. The main trouble was that, in addition to everything, I had lost the warm shawl given me by Klavdiya Ivanovna.

I lost it when we were returning from Divisional H.Q. to Army H.Q. We drove for a long time along snow roads in the forest. Later we had to get out and crawl across a piece of open ground on our hands and knees. It was a place the Germans particularly liked to shoot over.

A soldier who was sent to meet us ran next to me. He was breathing heavily, was mad with impatience, as he said to me in a whisper: 'You must be an actress from the theatre company? You will perform for us?'

And at that moment I felt sorry I was not an actress. It was so hard to run bent double over the snow, and I was so excited by everything that was happening that I dropped the shawl on the snow without noticing. It's easy to miss white on white.

We drove into Leningrad itself from the Rzhevka side. From the exciting, active life at the Front we came back to the smokeless silence of the besieged city.

27th February, 1942

Altogether we spent three days behind 'The Ring'. Having divided into groups our delegations visited all kinds of units. Our group was taken to the battery six hundred metres from the enemy, and this wasn't the most advanced position.

At each of these batteries, which are hidden in a wood, we held brief meetings. Everyone was standing. One of us spoke, then one of the gunners answered. We were surrounded by snow-covered pine and fir trees, and guns uncovered, ready to fire. There was only one theme in our speeches—the break-through of the Blockade, the liberation of Leningrad from the enemy.

One of the gunners said: 'Give Leningrad greetings from the first gun. Tell them that we are doing everything, so that the city of Lenin can rest from its tiredness.'

Another man said: 'It's possible to push back the German, but that isn't our goal. He has to be destroyed.'

The expressions 'The fighting man saturated with hatred' and 'Such a vengeance worked itself out in him' was said by the same man.

At one of the batteries a shot was fired in honour of each of us. The thunder of guns deafened us, the snow, shaken off the trees, covered our heads and shoulders. In a few moments the Germans answered. The shells fell wide.

During these three days with the Army we learned that the German cannot stand the smallest flanking movement or encirclement, and that his reserves are sparse.

We heard a story about a man who 'fled' to the advanced line. He was a barber by trade. In view of his usefulness it was decided to keep him at H.Q. But he was not properly supervised. He fled and is now 'shaving the Fritzes with his machine-gun'. But as a barber he is lost.

And there is the story of a woman whose son-in-law came on leave to Leningrad. She disliked the man and said, 'All the time on the wireless I hear talk of Fedyuninsky's men, Fedyuninsky's men . . . I wish I could see one.'

And the son-in-law answered, 'Look at me, honoured Mother, and you will see one.' And for the first time the woman called him her little son.

It was made clear to us that 'Should you transfer an officer to a soft bed and a warm room he will immediately catch 'flu. A commander needs cold, a dug-out and austerity.'

. . . A story of how a soldier was killed while distributing bread. A shell blew him to bits. There was nothing left of him to bury, but a hunk of the loaf escaped, soaked in blood. The soldiers buried this, instead of the man.

. . . A story about the greatcoats and felt boots placed near the camp-fires.

Tired soldiers, as soon as they manage to reach a camp-fire, contrive to stick a leg in it. A 'Komsomol' member* is placed on duty at the fire. He is deadly sleepy himself, but he must wake up those who fall asleep, so that they do not fall in the fire. And if he is not successful in waking up the soldiers he pulls their legs away from the fire . . . and a sleeping leg which has covered scores of kilometres during the day—you can imagine how much it weighs.

An observation by a major—'German ski troops don't as a rule go on skis. Are they scared of Russian snow or what?'

A workman from the coast regions, a former gunner—'As I heard the pill-box firing, it was such a pleasure.'

The 'correct' way to point a gun was under discussion. That is—who directs the gun barrel by swiftly moving its tail, following the instructions of the gun layer. An officer said, 'In war it's not only force that is needed, calculation is needed as well. Some hefty fellow will lift half the gun, whereas it is important not to throw over further than necessary.'

The head of the club who took us to the command post approved of my smallness which allowed me to walk without bending. German bullets here are aimed to hit a medium-sized person. This can be seen from the scarring on the trees.

A machine-gunner who accompanied us remarked sadly:

'After the war the lumberjacks will have a hard time of it.'

'Why?'

'The men will start to saw the tree-trunks, and in the trunks there'll be all these metal fragments, so that the saws will break.'

When we return from the battery we saw a group of soldiers. They stood in a double circle, surrounding a man who had a paper in his hands. The scarlet rays of the sun lit their solemn faces. We asked what this was, and it was explained to us that it was a military revolutionary tribunal.

* Member of the Communist Youth League.

'For what is the man being tried?'

We were answered briefly and sternly: 'For cowardice.'

At the entrance to one of the dugouts at the Divisional H.Q. we were given a warning.

'Go on—there are no steps here, only a ramp.' We went down. In the darkness, red and green lights glowed gently—two, two more—and in the background another pair. These were horses' eyes. One horse was nervous. The groom—a Red Army man—stroked it, explaining, 'It's only a young one.'

I thought of the bronze Leningrad horses, taken from their home by the Anitchkov Bridge to a place where they are safe from shells and bombs. Probably they too were standing in some underground hiding place, quietly stamping their hooves, and the bronze youth who holds their reins quietens them down.

We dined in the Divisional Commander's dugout. It was so warm there that in two or three places birch shoots were sprouting in the earthen wall . . . a fragile stem and tiny leaves, weak and pale but still alive.

At the beginning of dinner, and before all other toasts, we toasted Stalin, for his Order of the Day, calling for victory. The second toast was for the liberation of Leningrad. The Commissar said: 'To live or not isn't the question. Our life belongs to Leningrad.'

10th March, 1942

As usual, I am worried about I.D.'s work. What is going to be the end of all this? But more worrying and upsetting are Jeanne's letters. I get them frequently now, and they simply torment me. The most frightening are the ones that were written while the child was still alive. The post comes erratically; what was sent earlier arrives later. I still haven't received the letter about the boy's death.

Mishenka is no more, and I haven't even got a photograph of him, only the pink rattle. I have taken it down and hidden it in the table drawer.

12th March, 1942. Evening

A letter from Jeanne addressed to I.D. 'Towards the end of the day his little eyes began to squint, and he drew back his tiny head. It was meningitis and the first person to diagnose it was me. I had come across this illness once before in my life, and recognised it at once. At that moment I realised it was all over, and I wished for only one thing—that the child wouldn't suffer for too long . . . I shan't describe his last hours to you, I simply cannot. We used three oxygen cylinders in a few hours, and thus he died, breathing in oxygen, probably unconscious. We buried him in peasant style—tied his little coffin to a sleigh, and drove it to the cemetery. That's how we have become involved with this town that has given us a refuge.'

It is hard—well-nigh impossible—for me to read all this. Now I must work extra hard—in order to get a hold of myself.

22nd March, 1942

Yesterday, at exactly three o'clock, the shelling of our grounds began. We never even heard the whistles, just the thuds. Six six-inch shells hit us. Two of them damaged the single-storey building that is the kitchen. They flew through the roof, went through to the basement, where a young plumber was killed. Another boy, the son of a woman orderly, had both his legs blown off.

A shell crashed through the walls of the anatomy theatre, went through the auditorium (what luck no one was there!), blew the library cupboards to smithereens. It also exploded some specimens in spirit. I went some time ago with I.D. to look at these, but failed to stay the course. I remember I could face examining jars with 'Liver,' Kidney', 'Heart', on the labels. But then I found myself in front of a jar labelled 'Nose'. And half the head of a young man with immaculate features was suspended in a transparent fluid. I suddenly didn't feel too well, and I rushed down the stairs at such a speed that I.D. had difficulty in catching me at the bottom.

And now this dead youth has died a second time.

Two shells fell in front of our windows. Cracks by the stove in our room have got bigger. Everything shook. I stood with Marietta. We were in our fur coats and we didn't know whether it was better to stay or go. As a result of this shelling (or independent of it), the big kitchen mains were damaged again. I.D. is in despair. Even his invincible optimism has cracked, like our wall.

27th March, 1942

In a couple of days we shall move to a large room with three windows facing east. I can hardly wait. It will be possible to move without knocking into the furniture, and to be in the same room without breathing down each other's necks.

Lately, our tiny room, so nice during the winter, has become hateful to me. (The anti-aircraft guns seem to be in action; evidently a reconnaissance plane is above. Can it be that raids are starting again?)

Today is 'Working Sunday' for street cleaning. I.D. is there. I write and iron intermittently. Marietta is improvising at the stove. We have become miraculously rich—because we have received parcels from the Writers' Union in Moscow. I was bewildered when I saw all that had been sent to us. I grabbed a tin of condensed milk in each hand. I cannot bear to let them go.

28th March, 1942

Roentgen Street, quite near us, has been shelled. In front of the Roentgen Institute there is a statue of a bronze head of Roentgen on a tall pile of granite books. They are arranged as if an impatient hand is searching for the right volume.

I.D. told me that forty years ago (also in March) in a book-shop in the main street of Würzburg a photograph of a hand was exhibited, in which the bones of the fingers were plainly seen, and a ring on one of the fingers. The muscles, nerves, blood vessels and skin had disappeared, as if they had never been there. It was one of the first X-ray—'Roentgen'—photographs.

That evening, all the students marched through the city, by torchlight, carrying banners. They marched past the two-storey building of the Physics Institute where Professor Roentgen gave his lectures. And not only students, state officials, soldiers, merchants—all the people of Würzburg honoured their great fellow countryman.

And in March 1942 a German shell exploded in the street of Roentgen and damaged the monument. Marietta and I went to have a look at it. Some of the granite blocks had been blown out by the blast. The head itself remained intact, but it was lying on its side. And that is how it is lying now, on its side, mournfully pressing its cheek to the granite.

Melting and falling snow covers the high forehead with a cold sweat, tears roll off the cheek and hide themselves in the thick beard. I have written, for publication abroad, an essay called 'The Street of Roentgen'.

29th March, 1942. Sunday

We were wakened at six in the morning by terrific explosions. There were four of them with very long breaks in between. The earth and even the air shook. Is it possible that there are such powerful missiles?

Evening

We have just learned that in the morning trucks loaded with shells were set on fire by German bombs on the line near Rzhevka.

I am now doing very little work and this torments me. The poem has been pushed aside, scattered irretrievably. On top of this, the stove drives me mad. It is cold and it smokes, and where we shall find anyone to repair it and sweep the chimney, God only knows. It seems that there was a chimney sweep but he died a few days ago.

Now, in the days to come, the spring fate of the town is being decided. Will there be an epidemic or won't there? Will there be an infection explosion or won't there? It takes my breath away to contemplate typhus or dysentery in Leningrad. Which of us will have the strength to survive all this? And who will look after the patients?

The entire population of the city, everyone who is capable of holding a spade or a crowbar, cleans the streets. And that is rather like putting a soiled North Pole in order. All is chaos— blocks of ice, frozen hummocks of rubbish, stalactites of sewage. There are many volunteers. The *Leningrad Pravda* published an interview with eleven-year-old Fima Ozerkin from Ligovskaya Street. Fima said:

'Nobody ordered us to clean up the courtyard, we did it of our own free will. Have you noticed that the large snow mound in our yard is no more? That is because Tolya and I have cleared it up. Tomorrow we shall do some more clearing.'

We are moved when we see a piece of clean pavement on the quayside or on the bridge. To us it seems as beautiful as a flower-strewn glade.

And a yellow-faced, bloated-up woman, wearing a smoke-blackened fur coat—she can't have taken it off all the winter—leaned on a crowbar, gazing at a scrap of asphalt, cleaned by her. And then she went back to work.

A new idea in the city—everyone is carrying pine and fir branches. They contain vitamins, and we drink an extract of pine needles. The bark is sliced off oak trees, particularly the young ones, up to the height of a human adult. It is boiled and drunk in order to prevent stomach disorders. There is a lot of tannin in the bark, and this is a binding substance. But the stripped trees look like a human being without skin.

Recently, I saw an unbelievably thin horse in the street. But as it has lived through last winer, it is possible that it will survive.

Anything I do makes me terribly tired. What am I afraid of? Not the bombing, not the shells, not the hunger, but a spiritual exhaustion—the limit of tiredness, when one begins to hate things, sounds and objects. It's not for nothing that they say the people with the strongest nerves win. I'm afraid of this very thing—frayed nerves, emotional breakdown, degradation. Worst of all, I can't write.

I am going to bed, and what will be, will be.

30th March, 1942

The night passed quietly. I slept like a log, only bad dreams distressed me. In one dream I saw a little child with one enormous blue eye stretched right across his forehead. And the mother said, 'Well, you see, both his eyes merged into one.'

Thus the image of the little blue-eyed girl Kirochka was transformed in my dream. Yesterday I heard a great deal about her, saw her charming marble head torn from her body by blast. The same thing would have happened to the living Kirochka had she stayed in her nursery in Leningrad.

It is very cold in our room. The stove-mender dangled the chance of a visit before us, but he never came. In spite of this, I feel better today. Perhaps because the unsettling promise of spring has come to an end. There is a blizzard raging.

31st March, 1942

It couldn't be a worse day. One of the most upsetting of my Leningrad days.

Yesterday we moved into the new room. It received me with a terrible welcome—insomnia, and of such a nerve-racking kind. I had got tired, dragging our things about. We couldn't manage to move the bed, and I lay down on the sofa. Then I thought about Sofya Vasilyevna, now dead, who slept on it, and that kept me awake. At one o'clock at night the shelling started in the distance. It seemed to me, however, that it was bombing, and that because we had no radio we heard no alert.

And in the strange atmosphere, listening to those far-off explosions, I felt a fear as I have never experienced it in my life before, not in Zhikharevo, not at the Sitnoy Market, nowhere have I known anything like it.

I was shivering, I was freezing. And to make matters worse, I.D. was sleeping so well. I tried to wake him, and he only murmured, 'It's nothing, my dear.'

I gave it up and went downstairs to H.Q., but for some reason that was firmly shut. The night was as clear as day, what with the moon and the snow. I came back. Fluffy spring snow—the trees looked like apple trees, covered in blossom.

For the hundredth time I sat down and read a French novel. But reading seemed so unreal, like a dream within a dream . . . this life, those loves, somewhere on the Riviera, in Nice.

Nikolai Ivanovich came to see us and he reported that our students of the first two years are to be evacuated from Leningrad. The date—up to April 10th, while Lake Ladoga is still firm. The third- and fourth-year students will stay. I.D. will stay with them, and I will stay with I.D.

Nine o'clock in the evening

Order has established itself in our room, and with it a relative cosiness. But I have such feelings of uncertainty and of anxiety that I cannot find a place for myself. What will happen to us? What will become of me? I don't know.

I know nothing. I am distressed and very much afraid. I write about it without false shame. I AM AFRAID. Today Marietta told us that the Germans are very close to the city. Evidently I sensed this, although I didn't know it. They have brought up a powerful battery on a railway truck and shelled the city.

1st April, 1942

I am sitting down to write verses for the *Leningrad Pravda*. It is about a collective farm waggon-train which battled its way through all the punitive expeditions of the Germans. More than two hundred drays with food supplies arrived. All this went secretly across the front line. Yesterday, at midnight, I was telephoned by the editorial office, but I didn't succeed in seeing the delegation, after all, because of transport. Of course, there is no petrol.

The room is gradually becoming more lived in. Yesterday I spent a good working day in it, and apparently my zeal warmed up the walls. Outside there is a light March—no, April—snow. An excellent day for work. The sirens are silent.

We are assured that within two or three days there will be light in our building from a small mobile motor. It is hard to believe in such happiness!

4th April, 1942

A fierce raid. The first this year. Once again, as they did six months ago, the buildings shook: deafening roars. Professor P., who was on his way to me, with a small globe he had promised me, was nearly killed.

We stood in the corridor on the first floor. After all, it is safer there.

On the 6th April half the Institute departs for Pyatigorsk. At first there was a plan for me to go with them as far as Moscow, so that I can settle my affairs (enough has accumulated) and return by plane, but it turns out that the Institute party will not go by Moscow after all.

Now there is a possibility that I may fly there with Grusdev.

Yesterday I gave a talk to the 2nd Communications Regiment; though I spoke to each platoon separately, they listened well.

This occasion tired me very much. My forehead was damp, my hands began to go numb. I found it increasingly difficult to read. Then, too, the hall is singularly inconvenient, long and narrow as a fire hose. I had to strain my voice a great deal in order to be heard in the back rows. But there was complete silence.

After the reading I was led into the regimental dining room. I was delighted.

I was served a steaming deep bowl of soup, filled to the brim with pieces of meat. We hardly had time to put our spoons in our bowls before people came running in to say that a passenger car is going to our Petrograd district, and that if I miss it I shall have to walk . . . so I had to go. On the way back at a dark crossing a lorry nearly hit us . . . in our blacked-out streets this happens fairly often.

7th April, 1942

A very difficult day. It started in the morning. Nikolai Ivanovich came and announced a case of typhus in the Students' Hostel. I.D., poor man, was dumbfounded. All the time he has feared something like this would happen. But before that, Efrosinya had come and told us that her husband had died. I gave her a bit of bread (down payment for the coffin) and she left without lighting the stove. The Institute's upholsterer helped me to do it. He worked the whole day in our place, hanging curtains and dividing the room.

I fed the upholsterer.

The young girl Vera, who brings us our lunch pail from the kitchen, is being evacuated tomorrow, with the Institute. So another girl, Nyura, came instead of her. She was so hungry that I immediately gave her some porridge.

Yuliya Markovna Hefter came with a broken arm. Gave her tea.

Yuliya Markovna is a professor, a biochemist. She fell recently, slipping in the street. It's true she broke her arm, but the accident seems to have cheered her up; she doesn't want to leave with the Institute, and now she has every reason not to.

I.D. arrived. Hungry. Gave him dinner. The girl Vera came to say good-bye—hungry as well. Gave her some porridge. Poor tired and hungry Marietta (and I.D. hungry again) is yet to come.

Nevertheless, I managed to do some work. Our present room used to be a lecture room. I.D.'s diagrams still hang on the wall —the work of a country doctor, infant mortality in the first months, and so on. The room is large, we only occupy the part where the stove is. In the other part there is a collection of blackboards, writing desks, ink-pots and pointers. But in our corridor there are classrooms that are still in action. Now it is warmer, but the teaching went on there in the winter, when professors and students (all in fur coats) huddled round the stove.

Once, in the January twilight, I was walking down the corridor, and I saw a girl student alone by a lukewarm stove. She was embracing the stove with her entire being, her arms round it, her forehead pressing against it. She sat like that for quite a while, with her eyes closed. Then she moved to the window, through which the setting sun was penetrating, and once again she took up her book.

Also, in January, late in the evening, I needed urgently to look up in the *Big Soviet Encyclopedia* the word 'Leningrad'. I went down to the study where the dictionary was locked in a cupboard.

I walked into the study. There were the duty officers, a girl and a male student. He was perched on a chair near the stove. She (I didn't realise at first that she was a girl) wore a man's shapeless fur coat, a man's hat and glasses with thick lenses. She had the sooty lamp burning, as she prepared for her histolology test.

Marietta told me later that this girl had that day buried her father and mother together. Her father had died a few days before, but her mother had said:

'Wait for the funeral. You can bury us together.'

It is difficult with the patients. Water is needed and it still isn't there. They have sweated and strained over this for ages, but they still can't find out what is wrong. Is the water still frozen deep down (although everything is thawing) or has a shell severed the main?

8th April, 1942

A confused day, full of excitement. All night the Institute was getting ready for its evacuation. We intended to drive to the station, but at the last moment the car let us down. Neither did we say good-bye to Nikolai Ivanovich, or Alena, or anyone. The letters, after all, remained unsent.

I.D. is frightening. He limps, he can hardly walk. But the most terrifying thing is his face. I simply do not remember ever seeing such colours in a human face—ash yellow with bright red cheek-bones. I feel so sorry for him, I could cry.

9th April, 1942

A quiet night. And a quiet (in every respect) beginning of the day.

The Institute looks like a beehive that has been deserted by half the bees. There is no one in the lecture rooms of our faculty. Efrosiniya is burying her husband. I.D. has gone downstairs. He is leaning on a stick and can hardly move his bad leg. Everything is still.

Outside the window, a kind of simple, greyish sky. Everything is flooded, everything is thawing. Even some kind of bird is jumping from branch to branch, cocking its head, its chirps can even be heard through the closed windows. The snow is at its last gasp.

I.D. spoke well when he said that this spring, of all the life in Leningrad, only the plants will be sated up to the hilt, there is so much water about.

Yesterday I went at dusk with I.D. to the Students' Hostel where the typhus has broken out. I.D. refused to let me go in. He went alone, and I walked up and down ouside, waiting for him.

I crossed the Grenadier Bridge and came back. The city looks heart-rending. The empty streets, the ruins, gaping courtyards, half-demolished walls hanging in space, waste ground flooded with water. Solitary figures. Untidy, running spring.

Yesterday Lelya and Inna left with the last convoy before the breaking up of the Ladoga ice. Dina Osipovna is dead.

How absurd the words 'Ladoga ice' sounded last year at the beginning of May. We were leaving the lit, warm, music-laden theatre, where Ulanova-Juliette danced sublimely and Balabina shone in *Don Quixote*, drunk with the music, warmed by the charm of the movements. We waited, chilled, for the tram, and wrapped ourselves up, turning our backs to the wind. People were saying, 'Ladoga ice has moved and that's why it's cold.' And in my imagination a kind of festive ice ballet took shape, all silver and sparkle . . . it swam, swaying and speeding to the blue waves, and now . . .

Afternoon

It seems I shall fly to Moscow the day after tomorrow, in the morning. So much to do! So much.

10th April, 1942

I woke in the night, in such a state of anguish and anxiety that my heart nearly stopped beating.

I.D. can hardly walk, he looks frightening, and changes under our eyes, and so quickly. Things in the hospital are getting worse, and now, on top of everything, we have this case of typhus. It's lucky it's only a single case—maybe there won't be another.

But there is good news too. Our group succeeded in boarding the Ladoga lorries. They have been on the other shore for a long time, and we can be sure they won't have to come back as they feared they might.

I think I can hear my stove catching alight. Efrosiniya is still burying her husband.

The hospital is still without water. As they haven't got a plan of the water mains (not even the city Water Board can find one) our men in charge of supplies poke into all points and taps, warming them up with last precious drops of oil. Then it turns out that this wasn't the right thing to do, that as there is no water, a place of no importance whatsoever was warmed up. And how could it be different? It is as if one were to prick the human body all over on the offchance of finding one particular vein.

And on my desk there stands, desired and unapproachable, the small school globe that was presented to me. It is musty and covered with mould in the Arctic region. (It stood for a whole winter in a bombed-out unheated flat.)

I traced 'my meridian' on it with a crimson pencil. But when I shall get down to that again, alas, I do not know. Yesterday I only wrote two stanzas.

The thought that I may be in Moscow tomorrow seems to me the most fantastic of all fantasies. But it's unlikely that it will be tomorrow.

13th April, 1942

The portable motor is now the centre of attention. Should it work, the laundry would be unfrozen, and the X-ray department start to operate. Without that, a hospital is not a hospital. If it should start to work . . . but it doesn't work.

It's not only our technical department, but the Secretary of the District Committee, Zhigalsky, an electrical engineer, who takes part in starting the motor.

He comes here daily. Daily, I see through the windows a crowd of people proceeding anxiously through the court towards a place between the boiler house and the T.B. department—a shed where the unco-operative dynamo is housed.

They are gesticulating. I can distinguish small movement of the fingers—imaginary drilling pressure on levers, drawing in air. One man throws up his hands in despair, it is clear that some part is missing. A discussion is going on about fuel for the motor, its heat regimens, etc. Zhigalsky got hold of the necessary parts, he has got the local factories involved. He himself watches over the work and struggles with the dynamo.

15th April, 1942

I am still here. The season of floods has begun. There is a 'non-flying runway' and the planes are grounded. It is quiet in town and on the Front as well.

Our evacuation is over. It is now dangerous to travel over Ladoga ice. Now we are properly cut off from the Great Earth. The ice doesn't hold any more, the water isn't clear yet.

I sleep badly, the quiet kills me. The shelling has nearly ceased, at least in our district. Even our own planes aren't flying, evidently because of the flooded 'runways'.

At sunset I walked with Marietta along the Grenadiers' Bridge. Heaps of rubbish thrown down are lying on the Nevka ice. As soon as it thaws, the water will carry the rubbish to the sea.

Yesterday I read for the first time 'The Mysteries' of Byron, (Bunin's translation). Although on the surface it appears very different, I'm sure that the real meaning is exactly the same, and that is terrific.

18th April, 1942

The date set for checking the typhus case is past. There has been no other case, and the patient, a girl student, has recovered. I.D. never thought it was a case of typhus.

Today Marietta and I went to the hostel to check up on the state of cleanliness there.

The corridors, where there used to be runners and wicker furniture, are now empty, and mortally cold. A thermometer still hangs, as if in mockery.

We looked at random into one of the rooms. People were starting to hack a mahogany table to pieces, one of the legs was already blazing in the little stove. One student was engaged in the firing, another, who was sitting by the fire on the table-top, laid on the floor, was reading aloud. The students were preparing for their final examinations. They wore their fur coats and hats. The sun, cold, but already bright, lit up their faces, which were pale, thin and unwashed, for a long time. And they pass their exams extremely well, that is what is so amazing.

We started to search for the Commandant of the hostel, who is also a student, in his final year. We found him in a comparatively warm and overcrowded small room. He was sitting near the stove, wearing not a fur coat, but a quilted jacket. He was repairing a watch, making slow movements with his frostbitten fingers. Little wheels, watch hands, the tiniest of screw-drivers were laid out on the table.

The Commandant was suffering from scurvy. Evidently he was completely tired out by the noise from the corridors, and by the effort of hacking up the furniture, which was now beyond him. And so he has completely absorbed himself in this quiet task, at the stove, in the warm spring sun.

However, we did get from him the answers to all our questions. He even informed us that the students planned to organise a day when they would do all their laundry.

On our way home we went down on to the ice of our Karpovka, and walked between its banks with their mountains of snow and rubbish. It was just as well that we are so light; under the ice, under our feet, we could clearly feel running water.

Everything sparkled and shone. Our feet felt cold through the soles of our shoes, from the ice, and our faces were hot from the heat of the sun, as if we were immersed in a deep bath of heat and cold at the same time.

19th April, 1942

We visited the Botanical Gardens.

Tikhomirov and Kurnakov led me through the whole place, and showed me the dead palms. I felt very bitter that I hadn't seen them when they were alive . . . and I meant to, each Sunday! . . .

On one of the walls of the Botanical Institute there is a black line—the water-level on that terrible day of the floods of 1824 (the year of the 'Bronze Horseman'). The 'disaster' level of 1941 is much higher. It is above our heads, on the level of the tops of the perished palms.

Tikhomirov told us about the collection of rare tulip bulbs which had been dug up by hungry people to make soup. One of these people was caught on the scene of the crime. He was carrying the bulbs away in a gas-mask case. Was it such a 'crime' during a winter like ours had been?

Tikhomirov's story about a 'tank attack' repelled by him in 1941 was also a good one. It may have happened on the day that we were bogged down by the disorderly column of lorries at the corner of Pesochnaya Street and the Aptekarsky Prospekt.

It was one of the days of the assault on Leningrad. Only now do we hear about it. One of our tank units, pursued by German planes, needed cover.

The tanks were already at the gates of the Botanical Gardens, indeed they were entering the Gardens in tight formation. Had they progressed a little further, precious trees would be ruined. Such trees, for instance, as the famous Black Poplar, planted by Peter the Great.

Tikhomirov rushed to meet the danger. The leader of the column didn't want to listen to anything. Still the tanks were advancing. Tikhomirov shouted:

'This garden has been tended for two hundred years, and you will ruin it in a few minutes.'

This sobered the Commander, evidently visualising those two hundred years. He lingered for a moment—and to linger during an advance means a retreat. Turning to his crew, the Commander ordered:

'Turn back. The position is unsuitable.'

And the tanks fell back and placed themselves along the Nevka under the branches of the trees overhanging the garden fence.

We went into the main building which is devoted to the herbarium. It is one of the biggest in the world, and contains about five million plants . . . and a 'windrose', isobars and isotherms . . . trails of cloud rushing round the globe which hangs on the wall.

I approached one of the cupboards, chose a shelf at random,

and (amazingly) the plant of my youth was there—wormwood of the Black Sea shores—just *this* species of wormwood—for there are scores of varieties—a rare piece of luck, amongst five million specimens, to bump into a childhood friend.

My wormwood bore the grandiose name of 'Artemisia Indorata, non-scented.' This is not true. It does smell, though not so strongly as other types of wormwood. I stood in front of it for a long time. I came home, tired, but very pleased with Volume One of the History of the Botanical Institute.

22nd April, 1942. Moscow

I am in Moscow. Arrived yesterday, by air.

23rd April, 1942. Moscow

A telegram from I.D. The laundry and the X-ray department working at last!

25th April, 1942. Moscow

I am desperately tired. I remember with longing my deep leather armchair at the window facing the hospital garden in Leningrad. And I am very worried about I.D.

I received a telegram from Jeanne. She, poor child, dreams of my coming to Chistopol or of her visiting me.

My literary affairs are in a good shape, but on the 24th there was a big raid in Leningrad, and this torments me.

Yesterday I was with the Ehrenburgs. I was reminded of my youth in far-off Paris. I remembered an hotel room, a typewriter, the cosiness of nomadic existence. Light and dedicated to work.

Ehrenburg works like nobody else. He writes three articles a day, and in the evening drinks a glass of wine from an elegant decanter and smokes a cigar with the long blue ash hanging from the end. Then he puts on a yellow camel-hair coat, a blue beret, puts the lead on Buza, his Scotch terrier, and takes him for a walk. He goes on to the 'Red Star,' writes again there, and listens to Goebbels on the radio, abusing him for his Israelite origin.

He returns at 2 a.m. and next morning everything begins all over again. Occasionally, he takes Buza for a walk in the morning as well, before settling down to work. And it's then that I can see him from my window.

I, too, live in an hotel now. My flat is unfit for human

habitation. There is no water, it is cold, the roof either leaks or freezes right through and the main thing—there is no lift. So I am living in an hotel, like a foreigner. And sitting in a room on the ninth floor I can see down into the courtyard. There, reduced in size but clear to the eye, are the figures of a man and a minute tiny dog. This is not bigger than a vignette in a book.

Ehrenburg gave me a Free France badge. It is in the form of a stamp, with a pale blue background, a black Latin letter V (for Victoire) and, on the right of that, a little scarlet Gallic cock's comb.

15th May, 1942. Moscow

I find it difficult to write about Moscow, it is so different from Leningrad. And what other city now is like it anywhere? Only when I am here can I feel how dear Leningrad is to me, how close. I want to be there, to share my fate with it, to give it all my strength.

20th May, 1942. Leningrad

When we came back from Moscow the plane landed in Khvoinaya. A tanker came up to us at once, and our Douglas sucked up petrol for a long time through its narrow canvas trunk.

A cranberry-coloured sunset was spreading over the pine trees, and the dry scent of a forest in spring was so overpowering, I just wanted to go on taking it in. It was like drinking crystals.

We crossed Lake Ladoga in seven minutes. By now it was quite clear of ice, and only lines of foam here and there showed up the outlines of the ice floes.

We circled for a while over the Smolny Aerodrome before we landed. And then—silence, the special, indescribable silence of a besieged city hit us, transferred us at once from the atmosphere of Moscow to that of Leningrad.

Not a single passenger car could be found. We were given a lift by a lorry which was taking into town the mail we had brought with us.

When we came to the main road we were carefully checked by a patrol. We passed Rzhevka, destroyed by an explosion. We passed endless streets, in never-ending succession. It was quite chilly, and at times it drizzled. The night was white. The woman driver asked us to give her at least a little sugar for her child, but unfortunately the only things we had with us were tobacco and some bread.

I.D. was resting when I knocked at our door. At once he solemnly laid out some presents, kept for me, not to be touched. They were sent by the New Zealand Red Cross.

The place of honour was occupied by a large tin of plain, yellow, purple and mauve striped boiled sweets. They looked so bright and clean that it seemed a pity to eat them, although there was nothing in them but some saccharine and chemicals.

Now it is necessary to do a lot of work, to catch up the time missed in Moscow. There were many impressions and reunions. The day passed so quickly—I hardly had time to recover. It was difficult to get used to the fact that one could walk through the streets without fear. People listened greedily about Leningrad and never got tired of asking questions about it.

23rd May, 1942

A young woman worker writes to her friend at the Front about the spring cleaning of Leningrad. 'And on the 1st of May our city sparkled like a precious stone', and then: 'I gathered the girls together, and said, "To work to rule under such conditions is impossible. We have to do far more." '

Our hospital grounds have also been cleaned up and put into order. It has become unrecognisable. People say it is even better than it was before the war. Ancient rubbish heaps on the waste land have yielded to kitchen-garden beds.

In one of the buildings of the students' canteen a section of 'intensified nutrition' has been opened. A few of these places have been opened in every district.

Pale, exhausted, weak people (dystrophy, second degree), make their way here slowly, screwing up their eyes against the spring sun, wondering that they are still alive. Sometimes they sit down and rest, exposing to the sun's rays a bare arm or leg covered in scurvy sores.

But there are also people in Leningrad who can't walk any more, can't even move (dystrophy, third degree). They lie motionless in their flats, frozen through during the winter; even the warmth of spring hasn't the strength to penetrate there.

Young doctors, medical students and nurses visit these flats. The totally exhausted are taken to hospital. At present we have about two thousand beds for them in various blocks, including the former maternity ward. So few babies are being born, there are practically none there.

Both the diet canteens and the visits to the flats by doctors are at the suggestion of Zhdanov.

24th May, 1942

Once again I visited the Mendeleyev sisters at the Pediatric Institute on the Viborgskaya Storona . . . that long-suffering district! When shells fly over our heads towards it, we say, worried, 'Yuliya Aronovna is getting it again.'

And it's true that the Institute stands in a very dangerous place; to the left is a factory where mines are being made, to the right there are barracks, and, quite near that, the viaduct of the Finnish railway. All targets for the Germans.

The Mendeleyev sisters—there are three of them—are no longer young. All three are doctors of medicine who graduated a long time ago, once again, at the same First Medical Institute.

The eldest, Yuliya Aronovna, has been for many years the Director of the Pediatric Institute. It is her baby, her creation.

It comprises a complete little town, rather like our First Medical Institute. Here, healthy children are being tended and sick children treated.

They are supplied with berry juices made from their own exemplary allotments. They give advice and training to doctors on pediatrics.

There is a T.B. clinic, where, in a short time, the children improve so much that their mothers no longer recognise them, and even complain to Yuliya Aronovna that the child has been substituted for another. That is how it was before the war, but the clinic is working now, although the milk 'ration' has been drastically reduced: two hundred grammes of cream for all departments, per twenty-four hours, is the ration now. It is being distributed virtually by drops.

But soya milk and powdered milk, dissolved in water, are being added to it. Even in these circumstances the children look well, and some of them even robust.

Arkasha Fedotov was so weak and quiet last winter that a 'death certificate' had been made for him, as it seemed impossible that the child could survive. Now he is a pink, fat little chap, with the loudest voice of all.

Yura Zolotoy is also in good shape. His mother died giving birth to him, and his father, now at the Front, writes letters of gratitude.

In the light, airy nurseries the tables and chairs are in three sizes—minute, small and a bit larger, like in the fairy tale.

We went there in the morning, and during the night the Institute grounds had been badly shelled. The tops of the poplars have been sheared off, as if cut by a knife. Roofing iron was torn off and hung in pieces from the trees. Three thousand square metres of glass were blown out from windows, and these had only recently been put back after a previous shelling.

Yuliya Aronovna led us into a long hall with a double lighting. On the walls were portraits of Cuvier, Voltaire, Bonaparte, Newton, Rousseau, Darwin—it turns out that they were all premature births. Some of them were reared in a beer jug filled with sheep's wool, some in a cotton-wool sleeve.

'And who knows how many have died,' says Yuliya Aronovna. 'Surely there must be so many more of them.'

In the Institute there is a department for premature children that is the only one of its kind. A baby who weighed only 650 grammes at birth was photographed next to a small milk bottle which was bigger than he was. He won first prize at a baby show when he was a year old.

Such premature babies are fed by a special probe with a glass funnel. This probe is marked by a thread, which shows up to what point it can be lowered into the stomach. The distance is infinitesimal, but it cannot be inserted any deeper, because jaundice sets in at once.

The Institute laboratory (a shell hit quite near) was being put in order while we were there. Smashed instruments were carried out, splinters swept away, thick dust brushed off. And all of them had only recently been installed after a heavy winter.

During the winter there were minus ten degrees of frost inside the Institute. Work became impossible, everything was transferred into a small room nearby, with a stove, and there the most delicate preparations were warmed.

Amongst other things, the laboratory was engaged in extracting the pure linseed oil from their store of paint drying oil, by a chemical process. Yuliya Aronovna now had 180 kilos of this oil which was distributed among the workers at the Institute as food.

Now they are preparing for redecoration, and I wondered whether the inventive laboratory workers would distil the remains of the linseed oil back into drying oil for painting.

None of the children were harmed during the shelling. They were all lowered into the shelter on their little mattresses. The lights suddenly went out, and until they were fixed, the children, lying in the darkness, repeated over and over again:

'We are here, do not tread on us.'

During the night three children were born in the shelter, two girls and one boy—Victor, weighing 2,500 grammes.

4th June, 1942

Today we went with V. G. Garshin to visit Ilyin, the old cartographer, who is also a numismatist in charge of the Hermitage numismatic department.

His small room is on a lower floor of the Hermitage with windows facing the Zimniya Kanavka. As I entered the room, I felt a strange shyness—I seemed to be a schoolgirl again, and in a moment I should be shown a blank map and asked to name the tributaries of the Volga. Luckily this did not happen.

Incidentally, Ilyin's speciality is mountains, not rivers. It seems that mountains are the most important things on maps, and the most complicated.

The old man is eighty-six, half paralysed, and he supports his head with his hand. However, on the left side, which is not paralysed, the profile is still beautiful. He must have been a wonderful-looking man.

Professor Ilyin told us that he was transferred to this room at the very beginning of the Blockade, that a bundle of logs was brought to him daily from the most sacred reserves of the Hermitage. Electric light was always there on his writing desk. The power was supplied by one of the warships moored for the winter at the quayside close to the Hermitage.

I asked where the Professor's department was now, and he told me that it had been evacuated from the city as soon as the bombing started.

'Why then did you stay yourself?' I asked.

'Where would I go? I am eighty-six years old and my collections are eternally young. One had to think of them first.'

Then he added that he had had many offers to leave. People came and insisted, but he refused because of his own personal collection of antique Russian coins. Though it is not a large collection it is very valuable and is already bequeathed to the Hermitage. It has to be brought finally into order, and this is occupying him at present.

The old man got up with difficulty from a sofa made of Karelian birch, and with a shaking hand he opened a drawer of his writing desk. Coins and medals lay in rows, between layers of newspapers.

Amongst others, there were tiny silver coins, about the size of fish scales—one of the first Russian roubles.

I noticed a yellowish fifty-copek coin which was of a much later date.

Ilyin explained to me that this coin had been lying near copper. Silver is very susceptible, as are all metals. It is only pure gold that is not influenced by anything and always remains itself.

When we were saying good-bye, Ilyin sang the praises of his little room. He had deliberately refused to have a radio, so that he would not hear air-raid alarms and get worked up sooner than necessary.

Garshin and I left the Hermitage and walked slowly along the embankment, which was flooded with sunshine. I particularly noticed that the sailors of the nearest naval vessel (was it the one that fed the Professor with electricity?) wore helmets, as they manned the anti-aircraft guns. In the distance a tram froze into immobility on the bridge. The embankment was empty. Then we suddenly realised that an alert was on, which we hadn't heard, owing to the Professor's lack of radio.

I wrote, for consumption abroad, an essay about Ilyin. I called it 'Pure Gold'.

12th June, 1942

Yesterday, late in the evening, I.D. and I went for a walk. Silver barrage balloons rose lightly into the pale pink melting sky until they seemed to dissolve into it. The lime trees along the Botanical Gardens by the Nevka river have already begun to bloom. And their scent deadens the smell of decay from the rubbish which is not yet completely cleared.

In a little wooden house next to the Militia station, on the other side of the Karpovka, a gramophone was playing captured German records and young Militia girls listened to the music, hanging out of the windows.

As we got back to the courtyard next to the student canteen, we heard a loudspeaker broadcasting the latest news: the signing by us of a treaty of friendship with Great Britain, for twenty years, of the journey of Molotov to London, of the decision to open a Second Front.

We finished listening to the tail-piece of the news at the H.Q. of our air-defence centre. Here, gas-masks hang in the corner like game bags. On the walls there are posters showing various types of bombs. On the table, instead of a pen-and-pencil holder, there is a piece of incendiary bomb, fancifully shaped, and dropped into a red metal nut. In a corner an eight-inch unexploded shell that had fallen in our grounds—on the table next to it, another piece of shell, this one of later construction, with six sections. Looking at this shell one can make out which way these murderous minds are working.

Can it be true that happiness will come again? That mankind will wake up one morning and find that Hitler isn't there any more?

22nd June, 1942

The first anniversary of the war. Today the news on the radio is alarming. Tobruk has fallen; the Germans have driven a wedge into the defence of Sebastopol. On the Kharkov sector they have forced a crossing over the northern Donetz, but were forced back.

24th June, 1942

At last, at last, I have finished the Part Three of 'Pulkovsky'! I started it on the 14th March.

29th June, 1942

The radio is alarming. A Kursk sector has made its appearance. The Germans are a hundred kilometres nearer to Moscow.

30th June, 1942

The radio is grave . . . Sebastopol is holding out, but obviously only just. Today it suddenly became clear that we have withdrawn at Volkhov. I.D. says that we are in approximately the same position as we were in the autumn. If the Germans occupy, shall we say, Tikhvin, then there will be a second ring of the Blockade here, for us.

5th July, 1942

We have abandoned Sebastopol. People here say that the Germans have brought up tanks to Tikhvin. Evidently they are thinking of starting another offensive against Leningrad.

Evgeny Petrov lost his life returning from Sebastopol.

6th July, 1942

A year ago, at about the same time, I was seeing Jeanne off to Chistopol. I saw Mishenka for the last time in life.

8th July, 1942

Threatening radio. Things are bad with the English in Libya. We are already fighting for Voronezh. Moscow is again in danger. The situation in Leningrad is also uneasy because of a compulsory evacuation on a wide scale. A decision has been made by the War Council to move all superfluous people, and to declare Leningrad a military city, 'with all consequences pursuant thereto'. Yesterday I learned that all the windows of our first floors will be reduced to slits. And, strangely enough, this calmed me down. If it has to be a fortress, then let it be a real fortress.

I began to value I.D. more and more. When everybody is jubilant over some success he says, 'Too early yet.' But when anyone panics, he says, 'There's no reason for that.' He believes in victory with his entire being, but not only from wishful thinking. He *knows* victory will come.

He teaches me to be controlled and brave. Naturally, I'm still afraid when the anti-aircraft guns fire right over my head, and, above all, when the shells whistle, though this very whistle proves that danger is past. I.D. is much braver than I. However, outwardly I'm nearly always calm, and that, after all, is already the beginning of real courage.

Above, The Road of Life over Lake Ladoga. The sign says 'the more crossings, the quicker the victory over the enemy'.

Below, Food supplies being ferried across Lake Ladoga in summer.

Part of the fence of the Summer Garden. The
Fortress of Peter and Paul is in the background.

9th July, 1942

Yesterday morning we drove to the Karelian Isthmus, towards Lake Ladoga, to Volo Varvi, to visit our students who are building defence fortifications. Dachas, log terraces, small country seats—all are empty. Pre-war life has left this place long ago. On one of the pillar-boxes a pair of starlings were sitting, lost in meditation. It seemed to me that they were deceived by the emptiness of the box, took it for a starling nest and intended to settle down in it.

Outside the city, this July day was radiant. The profusion of flowers amazed me. During this year we had somehow forgotten about them. But the stringent smell of petrol pursued us, or rather preceded us, drowning the scent of the woods and the meadows. In front of us, an army lorry was speeding ahead, and the petrol cap was not driven home. The precious fluid was pouring out on the highway, and the road was deserted so that there was no one to warn the reckless driver to stop.

We wandered about for a long time until we came at last to the barracks and tents where the students were living. The place where the fortifications are was further on, so we went on foot.

Lake Ladoga shone brilliantly in the distance, against the dark green of the forest. Our new line of defence construction had moved that far! It is further away from the city to the extent that the city has pushed the Germans away from its boundaries, but speaking generally, the Blockade ring had its longest stretch here, even before. After all, Leningrad is not in the centre of the ring. In the Kirov works area the Blockade approaches us at close quarters, but here it is sixty kilometres away. This is our furthest distance from the Germans.

Future dug-outs and trenches, worked by the girl students, follow exactly the bends of a tiny river, overgrown with water-lilies and threaded by dragonflies. It can never have dreamed that it would become a strategic 'water boundary'.

Still from afar, I noticed something that looked like unusually large flowers on the grassy banks—mallows, lilies, sunflowers and poppies. They were really blouses, skirts and slips drying in the warm air. The girls wash them in the river, in order to wear everything clean after work.

The work is heavy, the ground is swampy clay. Stinging

midges hang in the air. Everybody is bitten all over and has sun blisters too. The shoe position is very bad. There is no drinking water. But the main complaint is why aren't their colleagues of the same year sent to relieve them after such a long spell? And also:

'Why aren't other medical schools working? Why only us?'

One first-year girl student, little more than a child, was particularly adamant in asking these questions. She was black-eyed, barefoot, her feet covered in clay, her nose was protected from sun-burn by a green leaf. Nevertheless, she was the first to shout, 'Well—enough talking!'—and she jumped into a hollow that was being prepared for a machine-gun nest.

These girls had exchanged spacious lecture rooms for clay mounds and ditches, where all tests are taken by army commanders and there is no re-examination.

After dinner a meeting took place on the meadow between the barracks. Everybody sat on the grass. The back rows were constantly added to by people coming from work sectors further away. An army unit arrived, very organised, and settled down as well. Logs were burning to save us from the midges.

We sat on a mound on a large tree-trunk. I.D. read a report. When he said we had abandoned Sebastopol a shadow passed over the faces in the audience. The news had not reached them out here. I.D. appealed to the girls of Leningrad, in the name of the fatherland, in the name of vengeance for distant Sebastopol, to do everything so that their fathers and brothers should win. Later I read poetry.

On our way back an unfortunate thing happened to us—we lost our way in the half-light of dawn, this permanent twilight. We had been driving for a long time alongside an interminable shooting range. Then came fields of barbed-wire entanglements. Skulls and cross-bones drawn on small shields warned us that this field was mined. Dead-looking bushes stood out. The air was still, everything seemed so old, so sombre, unmovable, looking like the remains from some past war. The forest let us through and closed up again behind us. We drove for half an hour, an hour. . . .

Suddenly Sergi Pavlovitch says, 'What if we're driving right into the German lines?'

I can't speak of my feelings. Even I.D. was frightened. The driver's hands were shaking. At that moment we saw an observation tower some way ahead of us. It was empty, and we decided that if we should not meet anyone between us and the tower we'd turn back and find our way out of this awful place.

But at the foot of the tower we met a patrol. Never before had we seen such attractive human faces.

It turned out that we were driving in the right direction. After our documents had been carefully scrutinised we treated the patrolmen to cigarettes. They smoked with great pleasure. Three small columns of smoke hung in the motionless air. We looked back at them for a long time, laughing at our recent fears, but we were still shivering.

10th July, 1942

My birthday! The only personal grief during the year—the death of Mishenka. Had it not been for this, I should have been completely happy—with the best kind of happiness—with my work which has proved to be needed in war-time. I could have said about myself, what a partisan said: 'We live well. I say this because it shows that life is good when its working days are filled with fighting.'

And for me, writing is my battle.

Tonight I am flying off to Moscow, and from there to Chistopol, to see Jeanne.

13th July, 1942

The city of Moscow and Moscow Hotel—Moscow twice over. The radio is threatening. I haven't heard it so far today but yesterday there was fighting at the approaches to Voronezh. I.D. is worried, though he still believes everything will be for the best. I, too, believe. But in what state will we (and all other countries) be, after this monstrous war?

Here, for the first time, I have heard first-hand stories about Chistopol, and was able to feel its atmosphere. I shouldn't like to live there. I feel more and more that Leningrad is the only place for me now. It is simpler to live there, as well. And I do not doubt it will be simpler to die there, if need be. To perish in a fire, in an assault or under bombs in a raid—would be a fine, fighting death.

Leningrad at present is indeed a fortress. We are the garrison, and in a fortress everything is adapted for war. And it is easier there than in, for instance, Saratov. (I am listening to the radio. It is alarming. We 'fell back on new lines'. Fighting is still going on 'at the approaches to Voronezh'.)

16th July, 1942

The radio is very grave. We have abandoned Bogucharovo and Millerovo. Antokolsky has lost his son, aged eighteen, at the Front. It is nearly certain that Altausen is dead.

Selvinsky, limping with a stick—one foot in a boot and the other in a slipper; gloomy (after Kerch). He is also going to his family at Chistopol, but by train as far as Kazan. When I go and by what means is not yet clear. I'm thinking of going by plane.

And the days are passing by, passing by . . .

Here things are troubled. People say that the Germans were flying in to attack Moscow, but that they were beaten back at Podolsk. It will be good to be back in Leningrad.

Today we are going to the Militia office to make arrangements for my exit permit. The weather is hopeless for flying— rain and a thunderstorm in the early morning.

19th July, 1942. Kazan Airport

I sit in the hotel at the airport. To be accurate, it is more like a hostel. There are several beds in each room. The weather— God help us! Incessant rain, cold, gusty winds. One doesn't have to be a meteorologist to understand why it is impossible to take off. Yesterday we landed perfectly, but we were late. All the western sky was flaming red, and I thought, That means bad weather. And that is what happened.

Besides bad weather, there is also tragedy here, at the airport. Yesterday a 'U.2' crashed, and the crew of two went with it.

Today the victims were buried. Flowers and propeller blades wrapped in scarlet cloth were taken from here to the cemetery.

Last night I was woken up by a frightening thunderstorm. Great crashes of thunder shook the building. A little evacuee girl who was sleeping with her mother asked, crying:

'Mummy, who is firing?'

And so I am but a few steps from Jeanne, but there is no plane and I lack the courage to go by boat: it takes too long and there are too many complications. Maybe the weather will improve.

Dusk

A stormy orange horizon under fast-moving indigo clouds. The sky seems to be in flight, all the clouds are fleeing in one direction. It has stopped raining, but what will it be like tomorrow? A little while ago, I went again to the airport commander, and got the answer:

'Tomorrow we shall go without fail.'

I haven't heard the radio, but I am told we have abandoned Voroshilovgrad. I noticed that it's easier to hear bad news in Leningrad than it is here.

20th July, 1942. Morning

It is maddening. After all, it's only forty minutes' flying time. It would have been better if I'd gone by boat.

But the morning is marvellous now. There isn't a cloud in the sky, they have all been dispersed by the wind. I shall pay the Commander another visit.

In the afternoon

I am still here. There is no plane and the weather is deteriorating every minute. A flight is promised for half past four, but somehow I don't believe in it.

I shall be taken by a 'U.2'. After all, there are no passenger flights from here—only for mail and medical supplies.

22nd July, 1942. Chistopol

I arrived here by air in the early evening. I was no longer expected. I walked from the airport through quiet backwaters. Gentle winds from the country were blowing. Many years ago I was in Chistopol during a propaganda tour in 1924. Little did I think I should revisit it and that in its earth a child of my child should be buried.

I was brought here by a tiny mail plane, piloted by a woman. The mechanic who sent it off was also a woman. The little plane stayed on the ground for so long that I feared we should go like that all the way to Chistopol, but then I remembered Kama was on the way.

In a 'U.2' you feel very exposed. All around you is air, wind, emptiness, no stability whatever. The air route was full of holes and hollows, the enormous sun was ready to set. We flew over

Kama; the scent of the meadows rose even up to our height in the sky.

The Commandant of Chistopol Airport—also a woman—was standing waist high in grass. She took our 'U.2' by its wing, as if it were a crane, and stopped it.

When we parted, I tried to give my pilot cigarettes, but it seemed she didn't smoke. I offered half a bottle of good red wine, but no, she didn't drink either. Then after a short hesitation I pulled out a new lipstick, and this my pilot could not resist. Smiling and embarrassed, she took it.

23rd July, 1942

It is painful for me to be here. I feel sorry for Jeanne, but I can't make up my mind to take her back to Leningrad. I myself find it difficult to get used to such peaceful conditions. Yesterday I saw from my window a woman with a child running along the street, and I thought, How is it that I haven't heard the alert? It turned out that a nervous horse had broken loose and frightened the passers-by.

It seems strange to me that there is no blackout in the evening. As a matter of habit I constantly sit away from the windows.

This evening is my big public appearance. I shall read the 'Pulkovsky'.

24th July, 1942

There were a great many people. All our friends in Chistopol were there. Muscovites who had been brought here by the war. In the Presidium, Pasternak, Selvinsky, Isakovsky, Asseyer. It was all quite extraordinary.

I was very excited. Not in my usual way, but in a deeper, more—can I say it?—responsible excitement. In a sense I was speaking here in the name of Leningrad. Everybody was expecting just that from me.

The gangways between the chairs—the window seats—all were full. The doors were opened wide. People stood there, as well.

Through the windows we could see a hot, dry, starry night. The windows were not blacked out. (How unlike Leningrad!)

I spoke and read well, though it was hard for me to read—particularly the third part, which is about the death of a child.

I stopped and remained silent for a short while, and in the hot silence I could hear the uneven, excited breathing of scores of people.

I tried hard . . . I wanted to break down the great distance, across half Russia, to bring nearer, right up to this quiet town near the Kama, the huge granite bulk of Leningrad, dimly lit by the white nights, now already waning.

I spoke about the people of Leningrad, about the women, the front-line soldiers, the children . . . about a boy who wept as he put out an incendiary bomb with sand. He was afraid of it, he was only nine years old; nevertheless, as he wept, he was extinguishing it.

When I had finished everyone rushed up to me, crowded round me, shook my hands. All this was bestowed on me in recognition of the greatness of Leningrad.

26th July, 1942. River landing stage at Ustye Kamskoe

Well—that's the end of Chistopol. Yesterday we spent the whole day on the airport, but there was nothing there for us to use, except the wonderful air, full of wormwood scent and the cold milk from the cellar.

There were only a few planes and not one would take us. I managed, by telephoning, to obtain a horse and we drove with Viktor Tipot back through the town to the river landing stage. We waited there from one in the afternoon till one at night, in the small clean room at the river station (these premises re-minded me of Peggotty's flat in *David Copperfield*). Then we boarded the ship. We shall be in Kazan in the afternoon.

28th July, 1942. Moscow

Back in Moscow. Our position at the Front is very grave. We have abandoned Rostov and Novocherkask, and something else grim is happening.

The journey was rather awful. I can't forget the limbless people; there aren't any in Leningrad. There there are injured people who can still recover.

At Kazan a young man on crutches climbed into the train with difficulty. A female guard repeated over and over again: 'Careful, careful, take care of your leg!' Her tone was full of pity.

This was a brand-new artificial leg, complete with shoe. It

was hanging on his back. The young man was also carrying a second (shoeless) leg in his arms.

There was just one pleasant moment during this trying journey. At the station at Kurovskaya, I think, near Moscow, something prompted me to walk up to the *Pravda* stand. And there I saw that they had printed the third part of my 'Pulkovsky'.

3rd August, 1942. Leningrad

Yesterday we flew here in convoy from Moscow. There were five Douglas planes, with seven fighters escorting us.

The bulky bodies of the Douglases seemed suspended motionless and equidistant—only their propellers whirled like puffs of smoke. The fighters flew above us. All the time, somewhere at the side from us, air battles were taking place, but over Luga it was quiet.

It is getting towards midnight now. It's quiet, with occasional gun-fire. I feel depressed. However, it is absolutely essential to tackle Part Four tomorrow.

4th August, 1942

The jealous and demanding idols of cleanliness and order attacked me on my arrival and frenziedly demanded sacrifices.

I brought them these sacrifices with many genuflections, libations of clean water and slow waving of a duster. The domestic tyrants then calmed down (but only for the moment).

There was constant artillery fire in the night—extra heavy at dawn. At present—quiet.

Taking all in all, and including Tikhonov's radio speech, we are advancing. Apparently it has been decided to push the Germans back from the town, specially as they are heavily engaged in the South.

In the South things are grim. In America meetings are taking place about the speeding up of the Second Front. The world is in such a state of tension that sometimes I, a tiny particle of it, feel my bones ache physically, as if this unbearable load is pressing on me.

What luck (a machine-gun quite near, it's surprising) that I didn't bring Jeanne with me into this active warfare. No one knows what is ahead of us. Only one thing is clear—that the inactivity on our front has come to an end. The volcano is smoking now, and glowing, and the eruption is ahead of us.

5th August, 1942

I still haven't got into the rhythm of work. The journey to town yesterday was both tiring and pointless. The only joy was that Lesyuchevsky gave me a proof copy of my *Soul of Leningrad*. A poor little book, on poor-quality paper, but still dear to me.

Physically, I feel awful. When I'm not working it is as if I come face to face with my ailments, and they all leap at me. In fact I have the feeling that it's only when I'm working that nothing bad can happen to me.

'While I work a bullet won't get me,
While I work, my heart will not sink.'

7th August, 1942. Midnight

The city is quiet and deserted to an extent that is shattering.

Even the kitchen gardens hurt. The vegetables aren't growing as they should, the cabbage seedlings weren't thinned out. So huge, absurd leaves are growing without any body. They have such a bitter taste that even our hospital horses refuse to eat them. People carry away these tragic leaves, these shattered hopes, in the tram.

Quiet. Even the shelling has stopped. How can anyone write in such a city! It was easier even under the bombing. And what is it going to be like next winter?

On the 9th Shostakovich's Seventh Symphony is going to be performed in the Philharmonic Hall. Maybe that will dispel all this quietness.

Things are as they were in the South.

8th August, 1942

A cold, grey, joyless day. I don't feel like doing anything. Went to town about tickets for tomorrow's concert of Shostakovich. Cold!

And in the South it's an inferno. The Germans are approaching Armovir. I.D. said: 'They still can be stopped.'

And this 'still' is freezing the heart.

9th August, 1942

Again the Philharmonic Hall was filled to capacity, as it used to be before the war, and before things got too bad.

The members of the orchestra and Eliasberg, the conductor, were obviously keyed up.

I listened to the Seventh Symphony, and it seemed to me that it was all about Leningrad. The rumbling approach of German tanks—there they were. But the shining conclusion is still to come.

Everything about which Tikhonov said:

> 'That life, as the skill of a master
> Should enter the rustling of leaves
> As Atlantic Ocean singing
> Into tunes of the Neva and Thames.'

14th August, 1942

I.D. was called urgently to the District Committee. Just now they telephoned again, asking him to hurry. This is worrying.

15th August, 1942

Last night's call from the District Committee was to check our readiness in case of an enemy landing party. Can it be possible that we shall see the firing slits in front of our windows in action?

17th August, 1942

We have abandoned Maikop.

20th August, 1942

We have abandoned Krasnodar, but in retaliation have bombed Danzig, Koenigsberg and Tilsit.

Yesterday I was returning home alone under a barrage of shelling. The shells (new kind and very far-reaching) whistled down so straight that I could have pointed out accurately the piece of sky through which they flew. It was as if nails were striking on a glass pane.

Some woman at the start of it said: 'Well, got mad again!'

That was meant for the Germans.

It gave me a feeling of great satisfaction to realise I had completely ceased to be frightened.

I go into our room, and there is I.D. standing on a chair. The shelling is intense, but with the help of our upholsterer, Omry, he is hanging a plate on the wall. The plate comes from our

Soviet Lomonosov works, and along its rim is the inscription: 'The Mind does not Stand Captivity'. Symbolical!

23rd August, 1942

In the streets a 'Tass Window' poster is hung on the wall. On it is my poem 'Beat the Enemy!'

24th August, 1942

I arrived here a year ago today.

26th August, 1942

A 'complex situation' has developed at Stalingrad. We are going to Kronstadt; Ketlinskaya, Bergholz, Makogonenko and I. We shall give a reading there.

27th August, 1942

Our troops on the Western and Kalinin fronts have broken through the enemy defences, and thrown back the Germans forty-five kilometres. Forty-five thousand were killed. Our gains are enormous. Things in the South seem to be better as well, at least they are no worse. And, after all, it was only yesterday that we were fearful for Stalingrad.

This announcement was broadcast. When the announcer said, 'In the last hour', I realised from the tone of his voice that something extraordinary was coming.

It is remarkable how a communiqué can change the look on people's faces. Today we all look as if we had been sprinkled with some elixir of life. Efrosiniya Ivanovna entered beaming.

'The Germans have been pushed back!'

Tomorrow we go to Kronstadt by motor launch straight from Tuchkov Bridge.

29th August, 1942. Kronstadt. The 'House of the Navy'

We waited for a long time at the Tuchkov Bridge for darkness to fall. Motor launches only move after dark, but this moonlit night was so bright, it could hardly serve as protection. However, all was quiet. Only occasional rockets shot up.

'Smoke-screeners' escorted us, sailing between us and the shore. Their little guns, at the ready, showed up clearly as black patches in the moonlight.

We sat on the deck until we got chilly, then we went into a

small cabin, where we were forbidden to smoke, as we were facing the enemy shore.

We arrived very late at night at Kronstadt, and were taken to the 'House of the Navy'. The town was flooded with moonlight and was completely quiet.

In the square a patrol checked our passes. They held their secret torches very close to the ground, but the tiny yellow beam of the torch was no match for the moonlight.

One is more aware of the war here than in Leningrad. The streets are even more deserted, and even more has been noticeably destroyed. The chestnut trees, centuries old, have been mutilated by bombs. In the street I met a woman carrying a child to hospital. The child hung over its mother's shoulder, its head and eyes were bandaged with gauze, its little hand dangled in the air. The boy had been wounded the day before yesterday during the shelling. It's not right for children to remain here. I would have them taken away, all of them to the last one.

I still have a picture in my mind's eye of the ship in which we spoke. In, fact it isn't a ship any more, but a fortress firmly grown in the water. Last year, German dive-bombers inflicted heavy damage on it. The communication links of the turrets were lost, and they fought like isolated fortresses.

When the Commander of the central turret sent a messenger with an order to the forward one, the man reported that this tower had ceased to exist, and that, instead, the city dome was visible—such a wide gaping space had been opened up.

A whole mountain of rusting, monstrously twisted iron was lying on top of the mole, near the ship. It had been removed from here after the battle. But immobilised as she is, she is still a threat to the enemy.

When her remaining turrets open fire we in Leningrad can hear them, and Efrosiniya Ivanovna says:

'Well, with God's help!'

Our reading took place in the wardroom, where it was warm, even hot, from the proximity of the engine room, and because of the number of people who came to listen to us.

The city as a whole is a real naval stronghold. There are very few women in the streets. From the yard of the 'House of the Navy' we can see a fish in one of the windows, stretched by splinters. It had been presented to an actress who had come with her 'front-line team'. She is curing in the sun this present from grateful listeners.

And listeners here are indeed grateful.

2nd September, 1942

If Kronstadt is a key to Leningrad, then Kronslot is a small key to Kronstadt.

It is a small island, skilfully built as far back as the reign of Peter the Great. It is right at the entrance to Kronstadt. It locks the entrance, and it is impossible not to pass by the island when entering.

Kronslot is so small that I think sea spray must cover all of it. One can walk round the whole of it in twenty minutes. We didn't see a single woman here. Local seamen jokingly call Kronslot 'The Island of Lost Bridegrooms'.

We reached it by a small motor launch. We read in a place that had such thick walls that no shell can penetrate them. After our performance we were taken to the granite parapet. We stood there for a long time, looking across to the other side of the Gulf. There, in the clear autumn air, half-destroyed Peterhof emerged, plainly visible. We could see the outlines of the palace, the dome, clumps of trees. The Germans are there.

One of the Commanders said:

'Never mind. The time will come. . . .'

We returned in the evening under a strong wind. Tomorrow we visit the Fleet Air Arm Pilots at the other end of the peninsula.

4th September, 1942

I have written for publication abroad an essay about pilots. Here it is.

ACE

The pilots' reading room was in a wooden house in the forest. The magazines on the table smelt of pine needles. Posters hung on the walls. One of them was a picture of a famous ace—Guard Lt. Petrov. A leather helmet framed a stern courageous face. By his looks, one would give Petrov about thirty years. Under the portrait was the service record of the airman—500 combat sorties, 50 air battles: shot down singlehanded 5

Fascist planes; assault flights 30, reconnaissance flights 40, repulses 36.

I said to a colonel, who accompanied me, I would like to talk to Petrov if he is free.

'You are in luck,' he replied. 'Petrov is free today. I'll send him along to you presently.'

When I was alone, I stood on the threshold of the little house and looked at the airfield, which was surrounded on all sides by forest. A flight of fighter planes looked like dragonflies in an enormous meadow. The silence was complete and only from the depth of the blue autumn sky came a faint sound of engines.

Time went on, and Petrov didn't appear. Two young airmen passed by, talking in an excited way; a mechanic wearing an overall went by. A very young blue-eyed boy with a dimple on his chin went by. A ginger dog who was with him ran up to me.

'Goebbels, come back!' shouted the young airman.

'Why Goebbels?' I asked.

'That's what I ask too, why?' said the airman. 'It's disgusting. It's given the bitch a dirty name and she even answers to it.'

The airman stopped by me. For a brief moment we were silent.

'I don't know what to do,' I said. 'I'm expecting to meet a man here, and I've only got a little time left.'

'Me too,' sighed the airman. 'I haven't much time. The Colonel told me to go to the reading room, but he didn't say why.'

'Excuse me, then!' I exclaimed. 'You must be Petrov.'

'Right.'

'An ace?'

'So people call me.'

Involuntarily, I looked at the poster, comparing the portrait with the original. There was a resemblance—but no closer than between cousins of different age.

'That's me,' said Petrov, 'only I look older on that thing.'

'Yes, a little,' I agreed, suppressing a smile. 'And forgive me —but how old are you?'

'Twenty-one.' He paused, and went on, 'I shall be soon.' And then I realised that the photographer, embarrassed by the extreme youth of the ace, had aged him deliberately.

'Comrade Petrov, tell me how you fight. Are you brave and heroic by nature, or have you disciplined yourself?'

Petrov sat down on a small tree-trunk. The bitch Goebbels stretched adoringly at his feet.

'I find it difficult to answer your question. Courage . . . heroism . . . I don't think about that at all. I fly out to beat the Germans, that's what I think about. And I do beat them. For this, I'm ready to do anything, and I'm not the only one. During the winter we usually fly in masks and goggles, they protect us from cold, but reduce visibility. So last winter we flew without masks and without goggles.'

'And who thought up this way of flying?'

'One of us.'

'Couldn't be yourself?'

'That's unimportant. What is important is that we are increasing our efficiency that way. During the winter we had a hard time altogether. Sometimes we never left our machines for days and nights on end. We even slept on top of the wing. The Germans were stronger than we were in the air, and whenever they flew they considered it their duty to fly over us here and drop their bombs.'

'And now?'

'Now they think only of making a large detour, of bypassing us.'

'Tell me something about some of your combats.'

'Recently I fought two Messerschmitt 109's. One, I cut down at once. The other I was leading on all the time, from one small cloud to the next. I would dive out, then disappear, dive out, then disappear. I drove him into such a state that he lost patience and made a major mistake. He gave me too much space for a burst, so I cut him down and began to move away. And suddenly I look round, and good God! Our pilot is dangling on the end of a parachute, and a man from a third Messerschmitt is shooting at the parachute with a machine-gun. Then I turned back and forced this one to scarper. I couldn't cut him down. I myself had been hit, and I had very little petrol left.

'And would you think a German would save his comrade in the same way?'

'We know, from evidence given by captured pilots, that for each of our planes they shoot down they receive money. Do you understand? Money. All the Germans have to do is shoot

down a plane and run to the cashier. And for one of their
parachutists they get nothing. That's the way they fight.
Skunks. Mercenary bastards!'

Petrov got up. His youthful blue eyes grew dark, and deep
furrows appeared at the corners of his mouth, the veins of his
neck stood out. The ace Petrov stood in front of me, looking as
he did in the portrait.

5th September, 1942

Yesterday, at dawn, we returned from Kronstad. We had spent a
week there, and given eleven readings, not counting broadcasts.

Our last evening was held at the 'House of the Navy'.
There were about eight hundred people present. The sailors'
uniforms made it all look blue, and the gold of their little
anchors shone. We were listened to with great attention.

Our departure from Kronstad late at night was not without
adventure. At first we waited a long time for the 'smoke-
screeners', as the Navy didn't want us to go without them,
but in the end end we had to.

But the main problem was a barge which our motor launch
was supposed to tow and couldn't. The wind was too strong,
it was almost blowing a gale.

Everything looked ominous—the late, waning moon, the
ragged clouds, the whistling wind, the pounding waves.
The big barge was ghostly lit in the fitful moonlight. Not only
did she refuse to let herself be taken in tow, but she pressed on
us with her stern or sides and threatened to flatten our small
craft against the landing stage.

During our journey she gave us a dreadful time, she even
went adrift and had to be caught in mid-sea. And the German
rockets on the other shore made things so uncomfortable for us
that we bitterly regretted the absence of the 'smoke-screeners'.
However, everything ended happily, although we were thrown
about by the heavy seas. Simply thrown off our feet. There was
a moment when some large pieces of equipment seemed to fly
at me from all sides of the cabin.

We reached Tuchkov Bridge at dawn. Everything glowed
pink. As yet there were no trams. Ketlinskaya and I started off
on foot along the Bolshoi Prospekt to our home. We ate a
huge meal, drank a lot of coffee and fell asleep. The land is
infinitely preferable to the sea.

Women melting snow to obtain drinking water.

Porcelain plaque made in Paris in 1809, showing Leningrad as it was in the First Great Fatherland War.

(from the collection of S.M. Wolff)

6th September, 1942

In the South, battles of unheard-of ferocity are raging. It seems that Stalingrad will hold out.

I am writing a song, 'The Hillock X'.

Couldn't sleep for quite half the night because of this 'Hillock', but, for all that, I finished it.

Today there is a quiet autumn docile rain, smelling of leaves. It is a delight to be writing on such a day.

Yesterday I went to the Botanical Gardens. Summer is taking leave of them with indescribable beauty. Dragonflies were flying over a small pond. Not a breath of wind. The trees in the avenues have all started to go yellow; rowan trees were reflected in the water. Sometimes it seems to me that Leningrad now must be one of the quietest cities in the world.

9th September, 1942

Yesterday was the anniversary of the first raid on Leningrad (when the famous Badaev Stores were burned). It was a year ago yesterday that we went to the theatre to see the Chauve Souris.

I haven't seen Fedya P. since then. He died of hunger. At first he still had enough strength to appear in the hospitals as a reader, and he was fed for his services. But later he became weaker and found it increasingly hard to move.

10th September, 1942

I re-started Part Four in a new way. In the South—at Stalingrad—things are going well. In Novorossisk there is already fighting in the streets.

12th September, 1942. Evening

We have abandoned Novorossisk.

The wind is terrible and there is danger of flooding. Even our Karpovka is rising in a threatening way.

It looks as if the fourth part is going the way it should.

13th September, 1942

The wind and the waters have dropped.

At the Front there were no 'substantial changes'.

Part Four is moving along, but I still feel apprehensive. As it has been said by Pasternak, 'The poem hangs by a thread'.

I don't read much now. When one is working it is important not to change books, but, as it were, to freeze on to one or two in order not to disturb the existing flow of thought. Otherwise one reads something new, everything becomes confused, and it's difficult to write.

15th September, 1942

On our way back from town we missed two trams in Vedenskaya Street while we were listening to Tikhonov on the radio.

It was an appeal to the Caucasus towards which the Germans are now advancing—a talk to the Caucasian people. 'Georgians, Ossetes, children of Daghestan . . .' Tikhonov reminded them of the words of an old song: 'It will be a day of such heat that we shall be able to count only on the shade of our swords.'

Many people stood in the dark Leningrad Square that evening, under distant gun-fire, listening to that speech.

16th September, 1942

We have moved to new rooms. There are two of them this time. Fate willing, it seems we shall stay here till the end of the war.

Yesterday I spoke at the works that are called after Max Helz. Boy craftsmen work there. They sat quietly and listened well.

When I had finished a youngster wearing a cap with ear flaps came to the podium.

'The best shock worker in the workshop,' the Secretary of the Party organisation whispered to me.

In the name of the whole workshop the boy thanked me. I asked him if he liked poetry. He was silent for a moment, and then replied:

'But that wasn't poetry, that was truth.'

The highest praise.

Going home across the Karpovka I was accompanied by two works engineers, carrying small torches. They are at the works all the time. They are living there, as their families have been evacuated.

A few days ago one of them did go home to see how things were. He lives in Novoya Derevnya, in a small wooden house.

When he arrived he saw that the house was no longer there. The furniture was all in pieces. Amongst the debris he picked up two or three photographs of his wife and child—all that remained intact. The engineer said:

'Now my entire home goes into my pocket, and I can carry it about with me.'

18th September, 1942

Two hammers are at work, a curtain is being nailed, and a little stove installed. We are preparing ourselves for the winter—our second winter in Leningrad.

20th September, 1942

Terrible fighting in Stalingrad, but it still holds out.

21st September, 1942

General von Kleist has been killed at Mozdok. The English have bombed Munich to pieces. Things are more stable at Stalingrad.

When the communiqués are better it shows at once by the expression on people's faces, in the trams, on the streets, everywhere.

24th September, 1942

At the Front—no change. Fighting in the streets of Stalingrad.

26th September, 1942

After a break of five months we have an alert which has been going for about half an hour. It's a good thing I managed to get back from my walk as I have neither an air-alert pass nor a gas-mask.

29th September, 1942

The communiqué is not good on all three fronts. At Sinyavin the Germans have driven a wedge into our defence.

The afternoon communiqué was somewhat better than the evening one.

30th September, 1942

Came on foot from the Writers' Union. It is a golden autumn, like last year. Once again I.D., also like last year, is snowed under with office work, plus various problems.

Our guns are never silent, and we hear a constant distant rumble. In Stalingrad it would seem like paradise.

Things in Stalingrad are grave. Not a word about Sinyavin. The communiqué keeps silent and only the guns are audible.

All the time it seems to me that soon something frightening must happen to Leningrad. All will be well in the end, but we shall have to go through something frightening.

Our two rooms in the 'microbiology' department are so cosily arranged . . . let us hope it doesn't fly into micro pieces.

Today new wounded were brought to our hospital. It is not known where they came from.

6th October, 1942

Sometimes it seems to me that I am the mother of a prodigious family. My children are the stanzas of Part Four, and I think of them unremittingly day and night. I keep coming back again and again to one child or the other. I will dress this one better than the other, and do something to that untidy tuft of hair. I shall wipe the third one's nose, and the fourth I shall get rid of altogether. I am constantly adorning them, cleaning them, washing them, ironing for them. My priceless little children are improving all the time in my view, and my dear little Part Four is growing and growing.

Our radio has broken down, and so I don't know what is going on at the fronts. Only one thing I do know for certain—there is no Second Front.

Grey and damp autumn—excellent for working. I creep into my little corner behind the cupboard and switch on the light—while we still have light. I fall asleep instantly at night, and wake up in the morning with a stanza half ready. As if in the evening, I put a little piece of dough into a magic stove, and by the morning it has baked itself.

7th October, 1942

Yesterday my 'Hillock X' was printed in the *Leningrad Pravda*. It's such a treat to see this piece, dear to me, looking so handsome, because of its large type and its good position.

8th October, 1942

Read Armstrong on the fall of France.

9th October, 1942

At the fronts the same unprecedented battles. Stalingrad is holding out. It looks as if I shall write an excellent part . . . if only it doesn't drive me mad.

A wonderful quiet amber day. There is some gun-fire, but it is far away.

11th October, 1942

Five counter-attacks were beaten off north-west of Stalingrad.

A captured airman said that large forces have been drawn up there by the Germans. Evidently they mean to make a desperate stand.

Sinyavino has to some extent drawn German troops away from Leningrad, although our operation there wasn't a success. But the assault of Leningrad, if such is proposed, has thus been postponed.

My Part Four is moving along, but who is going to read it? Is poetry needed now, in these days of grim fighting?

14th October, 1942

For the third day running there are 'no changes' at the Front. Can it really be true that the Germans have been stopped? One is afraid to believe, one doesn't dare to hope.

15th October, 1942

On all fronts—'No substantial changes'. A big speech on the radio by Roosevelt, on the 400th anniversary of the discovery of America. A speech full of confidence in victory.

16th October, 1942

The Germans, having re-grouped their forces, it seems, have once again thrown themselves against Stalingrad and Mozdok. Mainly—Stalingrad. There they have thrown the might of their forces against the workers' settlement. They have succeeded in driving us back a little.

Now everything is decided at Stalingrad—the whole fate of the war. Today at noon there are bound to be important announcements.

Afternoon

The morning announcements were not good. The Germans have occupied a few streets in the workers' settlement.

17th October, 1942

The communiqué is very bad. We have given up the workers' settlement. Once again my heart is so heavy it is difficult to breathe.

I'm only at peace when I'm completely engrossed in work. Then suddenly my heart gets a jolt and I'm back again with all the troubles driven to the surface.

18th October, 1942

The communiqué is somewhat stiffer. We have repelled the attacks.

19th October, 1942

I feel increasingly worse in the mornings. Its harder than ever to get up. But one can't be ill now.

20th October, 1942

Yesterday I reached a state of complete exhaustion on account of the Jubilee poem. Then suddenly I reached a decision and chopped off the first two stanzas. These were the ones that were confusing me, but I had got attached to them and wouldn't let them go. Today I finished this poem.

It was a lesson to me not to be obstinate. Sometimes it happens that you take the wrong path. You can see it's wrong, but still you go on. And you plunge ever deeper into the mistake; its like going into a forest. And after all you should have dropped everything and gone off in a different direction.

Now I can tackle the Part Four. I was so overjoyed that everything had unravelled itself that I did some household chores.

27th October, 1942

At last! I can hardly believe it myself, but Part Four is finished —or rather nearly all of it has been rewritten, expanded here and shortened there.

But it was a heroic labour. I had almost decided to put away the poem and work on some small verses. I even began one such verse, and then suddenly decided to take the plunge, and I burned all my little boats—left the verses and attacked Part Four. And how I did it! I got myself into a strange state. I felt as if I were floating above the floor—levitating in a trance— if I had wanted to dust the room I could have done so as I floated by, it would only have needed a little more will-power.

Events swim by, leaving me practically untouched. In a dream-like state I received important guests from Moscow. They were visiting the Institute, and I gave them coffee and altogether did everything expected of me as a hostess. I have also attended to my teeth. The one thing I omitted was my English study. I had to rest my brain.

At the Front—no change. But now Tuapse has made its appearance And there is still no Second Front!

30th October, 1942

Part Four is a success. Read it again at the meeting of Baltic Writers. Now it only remains to write the fifth part and the year will not have passed in vain.

2nd November, 1942

Yesterday graduation evening was held in the large hall of our District Committee. It went off splendidly. But how I.D. fussed over it all! I also made an appearance.

Evening

I was watching a small children's stereoscopic panorama —the 'Pulkovo Observatory'—when there was a sudden crash. We thought it was a shell but it turned out to be a bomb, dropped before the alert sounded.

Eleven o'clock and forty-five minutes. All Clear. But I was too nervous to undress and lie down. It's better to wait a little longer.

3rd November, 1942

We have given up Nalchik.

The battle for Stalingrad goes on. The Press of the entire world is full of it. An Arab reporter writes: 'The fighting in the streets of Stalingrad secures peace in the Streets of Cairo, Alexandria, Beirut, Damascus and Bagdad.'

Twelve minutes to four

An alert.

8th November, 1942

Just finished the traditional post-holiday cleaning. I put everything in order, dusted everywhere, sorted out papers, drank a
cup of tea. And now ordinary working days have begun again.
I would call them 'dear working days'.

It really is curious why a celebration never turns out successfully for me. Is it that I'm not adaptable enough to catch the
spirit of it? Is it that I expect too much from it for myself and
it seldom comes up to my expectations? Or is it that during
celebrations one loses the habit of working?

I have been thinking lately a great deal about a play. If one
should write a play about Leningrad it would be good to take
some definite span of time—for instance, the duration of an
air raid from the alert to the All Clear—and what happens during
that time. This is good because one is already given an arbitrary
form, the beginning and the end are there, so there is no need
to invent them. Also, I am always attracted by the old-style
continuous action in conjunction with the variety of locality,
purely contemporary.

Or such a plot—a delayed-action bomb hits a house (as
happened with the 'Ars' cinema). Or it is presumed that it was a
delayed-action one. How do people behave? The bomb explodes
or it doesn't—that is according to what I, as the author, will
decide.

In Stalingrad fighting goes on in the factory district.

Is there in all the world a city spiritually closer to Stalingrad
than Leningrad? They call to each other over the hill-tops and
forests, above meadows and rivers. All the time they feel for
each other and the fate of one echoes hotly in the heart of the
other.

9th November, 1942

When I told Efrosiniya Ivanovna that the Germans have been
stopped near Stalingrad she answered:

'Oh, Vera Mikhailovna, it makes me tremble all over to hear
such things.'

I understand her very well. When I hear that the Germans are being beaten I too shiver all over with happiness. At times I pray I shan't die of joy on the day the Germans are finally beaten.

Heard only the second half of Stalin's radio speech, as there was a meeting at the 'Red Army House' at the same time. But as soon as the meeting was over we ran into the office of the head of the club. The reception was remarkable. It was as if Stalin were speaking in the same building, in the hall that we had just left.

There is something irresistible about Stalin's voice. You can feel from the sound of it that its owner knows everything, and that he will never be a hypocrite.

In this speech he spoke calmly and confidently about our relations with our allies, about victory, that is indisputable. Nobody doubts it, the only question is when it will happen. But after this speech even the 'when' has become somehow nearer. I live only to see this day!

Every day we have several alerts and quite heavy raids.

Yesterday I went to the first performance of *The Sea Stretches Wide,* written by Vishnevsky, Kron and Azarov, in collaboration.

It is a musical melodrama, and although from time to time the authors split asunder, as it were, in the presence of the audience, the piece as a whole is gay and vital. Yanet is simply marvellous, As a type he is clearly a find.

In the interval I heard a conversation between two girls from different offices, discussing the best place to see in the New Year. One said:

'We have a good band.' The other replied:

'And we have a better shelter.'

When we returned home and were drinking tea as we listened in a mood of relaxation to Rommel's *débâcle,* a raid started, and turned out to be very heavy. The German planes were somewhere pretty close. Our anti-aircraft guns boomed so loudly that they drowned all our voices. A lot of shrapnel fell in our grounds. We could hear it drumming on the roof.

The second run of the raid began quite soon. By the sound of the engines we could hear when the Germans began a new round, passing right over our heads. It lasted until half past one in the morning, and many bombs were dropped.

Last year, the raids went on until December. Probably it will happen again this year, and today is only the 9th November. We have a long way to go.

11.40 in the evening

An alert. And bombs at once, falling quite near. Our anti-aircraft battery is firing very heavily. And the evening was so quiet and domestic. We moved the furniture into different positions. We have had to move into my small room for the winter, as the large one is too cold . . . (At present things are quiet; we wait for the second part of the raid.)

After one at night

There was indeed a second part to the raid. And a heavy one. The interval between the two raids was about twenty-five minutes. Our anti-aircraft guns were simply beside themselves. Now there is complete silence, but as yet no All Clear. Evidently the German programme is—two raids at the minimum, one in the day, one at night. The day raid can be expected around noon, the night one at midnight. They will wear us all to a frazzle.

10th November, 1942

I'm afraid that these sleepless nights will wear me out to such an extent that I shan't be able to write at all. I dream all the time of submerging myself completely in Part Five, leaving only a chink for air.

Midday, and a few minutes after

I just had time to listen to the beginning of the news on the radio when the alert sounded.

However, I did manage to hear that we are 'crushing small groups of the enemy' in Stalingrad, and repelling their small attacks.

In North Africa the rout of the Germans, or rather of the Italians, is growing.

11th November, 1942

Bulatov, head of the Institute H.Q.'s air defence, quoted the words of a friend of his (a prominent soldier). He reported that the increased enemy activity on our front is explained by the change in the German Command here.

Infuriated by the failure of the Ladoga landing, and by the

Sinyavin operation, Hitler has appointed a new general. I don't know his name, but our 'new broom' is doing his best.

12th November, 1942

Finally settled down for the winter in my little room. I have moved the sofa in here, the dining table and the bookstand with the china. Even a fly kept itself alive near the stove—when it is warm the fly is lively and mobile, but when Efrosiniya Ivanovna fails to heat up the stove properly the fly sits listlessly on the wall. It takes the place of a thermometer for me.

The night was quiet. And it is still quiet. We don't know what is going on in North Africa, because the Germans take care not to let us listen to the foreign news on the radio. As soon as we come to it, there is an alert. But never mind—the Germans are being beaten in Libya, and that is authentic.

Evening

The Germans have landed at Tunis. Besides that, they have occupied Marseilles, Vichy, Lyons. Now the whole of France is in their hands.

In Stalingrad fighting is going on, street for street, house for house, staircase for staircase.

I can imagine what is going on in the ether now, what a jumble of radio waves, speeches, reports, communiqués, telegrams and so on!

So far as I'm concerned, I must write Part Five without pausing, otherwise it will be impossible to catch up with all that is happening.

14th November, 1942

What is the chief danger in writing poetry? Not to be tempted by irrelevant details, just because it's such a pleasure when your pen does what you want it to do. Now these details do not let themselves be caught, now they lure you with sudden flashes of inspiration. They show themselves at their most desirable, stand like supplicants at the edge of a poem or a novel: only open the door to them a crack—and they will pour in. But that is something one can't allow.

19th November, 1942

I.D. has again had so many problems with his winter schedule that he has started to suffer from insomnia. (An unheard-of thing for him.) He even asked me to give him Balderian with lilies of the valley before bedtime. I gave him some to drink and had some myself as well. Depressing thoughts have simply got the better of me. How shall we get through the winter?

20th November, 1942. One o'clock in the afternoon

On the radio a great success at Ordzhonikidze. Five thousand Germans were killed, almost three times as many wounded. A great deal of equipment captured. Things are good, too, with the Allies. They are approaching Bizerta. (A heavy shelling is over. It was near, too. But as if to compensate there hasn't been a raid for a long time.)

22nd November, 1942

A 'Special Announcement' on the radio. Our troops at Stalingrad have switched over to the offensive. It started from two directions, north-west and south. We have advanced sixty to seventy kilometres and occupied Kalach. And the most important thing, these words: 'The advance continues'.

Maybe this is indeed what is called the turning point of the war.

Four o'clock at night

Heavy shelling of our district has just stopped. Shells exploded nearby. In number 10, a neighbouring house, a woman was killed by a piece of shrapnel that flew through the window. We were at H.Q. when a medical orderly was sent from there to this flat, but the woman was already dead. We had come down to H.Q. because we were frightened in our bird's house. The whole place shook.

The night was indescribably beautiful. The light was throughout pink. I've noticed that the blue moonlight and white snow create a pink glow between them.

We heard twelve to fifteen salvoes at intervals of between fifteen and twenty minutes—the ration for our district.

Apparently a very heavy 'Sebastopol' gun was firing—obviously retribution for Stalingrad.

23rd November, 1942

As we expected last night, a raid began immediately after the shelling. I heard the anti-aircraft guns through my sleep, and then I heard nothing more. But one thing is obvious: now that the Germans are so angry over the fiasco at Stalingrad, one can't take any sleeping pills, one must be on the alert all the time.

24th November, 1942

Brilliant success at Stalingrad.

Afternoon

A story told by Z. V. Ogloblina. A patient in one of the wards says to her: 'Doctor, I look upon you as God'—'Or as a kilo of bread,' another corrected.

25th November, 1942

Last night, when we were asleep, there was a knock on the door. Bulatov appeared and reported that the waters of the Karpovka had risen alarmingly and flooded the area in front of the Botanical Gardens. If the wind rises, flooding is inevitable, but there is no wind today. A little snow has fallen. I don't know how the Karpovka will behave today.

The Germans will not let us listen to the radio. One can go mad.

26th November, 1942. Morning

Listened to the radio. Our offensive at Stalingrad continues. Another fifteen thousand prisoners, and six thousand killed—and that only brings us up to the 25th of this month.

The Allied situation is middling. The 'unrest' in Italy (how can they not be restless!) is interesting. Questions in the English Parliament about Darlan.

Here the night was very quiet. Air raids on Leningrad don't work out for the Germans. Things are different from last year!

3.30 at night

Just now I heard that Sergei Pavlovich, secretary of our Party Organisation, stopped Ilyin in the corridor and asked him:

'Was that shrapnel or what?' And Ilyin replied:

'Oh God knows, to hell with it!'—and then they proceeded to talk of the business on hand.

I can well understand this. When one is very busy and knows that the work is important, one isn't so frightened, and just doesn't think of the danger.

27th November, 1942. Morning

It is colder today. The houses are pale pink in the sun's reflection, and above them, looking cold, the late moon is still there in the morning. She looks like a guard who has been on duty all night, shrunk with cold, and ready to flop down to sleep on some tattered but warm cloud.

Afternoon

At Stalingrad we have taken twelve thousand more prisoners, thus the total is sixty-one thousand. The Germans are being driven towards the Don. Can it be that we shall have the joy of living to the end of the war?

28th November, 1942

No 'Special Announcement', but we are moving forwards. We are squeezing the Germans out of Stalingrad in district after district.

The Germans have entered Toulon, but the French fleet blew up all its ships: battleships, heavy and light cruisers, destroyers, twenty-five submarines. According to a report: 'In the morning the harbour was a shattering sight, all the ships were lying on their sides.' One can imagine this! But it's good that they didn't fall into Hitler's hands.

In Africa it is evident that the decisive battle for Bizerta is near. It would be nice to see the New Year in, if not with victory, at least with confidence of approaching victory.

The *Pravda* leader of the 25th November is headed: 'Leningrad, Odessa, Sebastopol, Stalingrad'. Medals for the defenders of these four cities will be struck. I am overcome with pride when I think that one of these cities, Odessa, is my home town, and that I myself am in Leningrad.

29th November, 1942. Morning

Our radio isn't working, so a man on duty at the air defence centre was sent to us yesterday, soon after one in the morning.

He came to deliver a 'Special Announcement'. We have broken through the German defence on the central front at Rzhev.

I read these words, written on a scrap of paper, in an icy room, lit by a paraffin lamp (there is no electricity at night). We lay awake, from sheer excitement, for the rest of the night.

Midnight

'Special Announcement'—Our advance continues both on the central front and at Stalingrad, where one more German defence line was broken.

30th November, 1942

An excellent article by Vassily Grossman in *Pravda* of the 26th: 'The Direction of the main Thrust'. I have cut it out and put it away.

Midnight

'Special Announcement'. Our offensive continues. In one day, at the central front, the Germans lost seven thousand killed.

7th December, 1942. A quarter to two in the morning

Finished, just finished, the poem.

16th December, 1942

'Pulkovsky' is already type-set and even the cover is ready. Tomorrow I'm going to have a look at it.

17th December, 1942

Today, when I came back from the Writers' Union, I asked I.D. whether I could apply for membership to the Party. For myself, I decided a long time ago that I would do it as soon as the poem was finished.

I.D. tells me that our Institute's Party Organisation is well disposed towards me.

18th December, 1942

The Party Committee is now in session. I have sent in an application for membership. S. P. Ivanov, Zhirmunskaya and Dimitriyeva have recommended me. They are all workers at our Institute, people with whom I have lived since I came here. I shall be called in presently, and I shall tell them the story of my life.

23rd December, 1941

Yesterday I was accepted as a candidate for Party membership.

Our offensive has begun in the middle reaches of the Don.

29th December, 1942

I am worried about Part Five. It's obvious that, after all, I've been over-subtle with it. As that slick character K. said, 'It's a very smart piece of work.' God save me from such praise.

On all the fronts our position is excellent. The Germans south of Stalingrad have been thrown back twenty-five kilometres.

The medals for the defenders of our four cities have been described, and pictures of them published, in *Pravda*.

1st January, 1943

Yesterday, late in the evening, we were putting the finishing touches to our supper table, for the New Year's Eve celebrations. It was light and gay, with pirozhkis and wine. Nearly all the guests had arrived, and we were waiting only for Vishnevsky, who was speaking on the radio. The communiqué began, summing up our six weeks' advance at Stalingrad. (Marietta and I froze so that the glasses in our hands shouldn't clink.)

The Germans have lost one hundred and seventy-five thousand; a hundred and thirty-seven thousand killed, thirty-seven thousand six hundred and fifty taken prisoner. We have surrounded twenty-two of their divisions.

Our first toast was to the Commander-in-Chief—the second to the Red Army.

2nd January, 1943

The last day of the old year didn't go by the way I wanted. I meant, on the last day, to make a short survey of my achievements, of my failures, and a list of my hopes, but I failed to do this. And today I haven't found time to write about it at all, and the day before yesterday I had no time to write after an air raid which lasted all night. A bomb fell not far from us and everything in our place shook. I don't seem to find time for anything.

We visited the fir tree* in the second surgical ward. I was on the point of reading to the patients when all of a sudden I myself felt ill. I am very tired.

I am worried by Part Five. People neither understand nor like it. That means I haven't said what I wanted to say. Can it be that I've spoiled the poem with a poor ending? And the ending must crown the work.

I'd like either to write something big or to take a rest . . . and read. I read so little now.

Well! I've complained enough, and cried on everyone's shoulder.†

Enough of it.

6th January, 1943. Somewhere about nine in the evening

I came recently back from the eleventh block therapeutical department, where a fir tree has been decorated for the medical personnel. There are some beautiful girls amongst the orderlies, real flourishing youth, ready to conquer and overcome everything. And to think how they looked last winter.

At the fir-tree party we had black coffee, with Dulcine— something like saccharine, but a pleasanter taste—and slices of black bread with glucose sprinkled on it. It looked like cottage cheese, and I thought it was tasty.

As a slimming diet it is good. Afterwards I felt a desire to write prose.

7th January, 1943

Yesterday night was stormy: alerts right up to the morning. The Germans dropped whole batches of incendiaries. A huge incendiary bomb was dropped near us—a whole cylinder filled with naphtha, and various inflammatory mixtures on top of it.

Our position at the Front is marvellous. We have taken Nalchik.

* Soviet substitute for a Christmas tree. Sometimes called the New Year's Tree.
† In Russian: 'to cry into someone's waistcoat'.

9th January, 1943

Had an amusing conversation with I.D. He said that a direct hit from a bomb is as rare as a win of two hundred thousand roubles, and so there is no need to be scared of it. This seemed convincing to me, but having thought it all over in the night, I asked him in the morning:

'Well, all right, a large win is rare, but small wins, like bomb fragments, are not at all that rare, surely?' I.D. agreed with me.

14th January, 1943

Too much happened today. Finished poems. Went to the printing works named after Volodarsky to be photographed for a newsreel. Ran into shelling twice.

At the printing works my picture was taken next to the linotype machine where my 'Pulkovsky' was set. I asked one girl worker:

'What were things like here, last winter?'

She replied:

'Just as you, Comrade Inber, described in your Part Two.'

Things are starting to happen on our front at Kolpino. One more attempt, and this time a serious one, to break through the ring. And the hard-pressed Germans raid us and shell us all at the same time.

At present there is an alert on, but it is quiet. The anti-aircraft guns are silent, but shells are falling near, and the radio announces that it is in our district. I do not know what to do—should I lie down? I am very tired, but pleased and happy.

If only we can succeed on our front. What a pity it would be to be killed just now!

16th January, 1943

An extraordinary day. The entire city is waiting . . . any moment now! We have taken Schlisselburg—that is true, but people are saying that both our fronts—the Leningrad and the Volkov—have linked up. Officially, nothing is known, but the city waits. . . .

Somewhere the guns are booming. An alert is just over. The way of life in a besieged city goes on, but everyone is waiting. Nobody says anything about it, nobody dares to in case a wrong word gets to wherever our fate is being decided, and changes it all.

I'm perplexed and bewildered. I can't find a place for myself. I try to write and fail. Went to the District Committee to have my photograph taken for my candidate's membership card.

Suppose that suddenly a 'Special Announcement' will be about us?

12.30 at night

One can't listen to this 'Special Announcement' calmly. Liberation is on the way!

18th January, 1943

'Special Announcement'. The Blockade has been broken. Leningrad is free.

19th January, 1943

Last night, immediately after the 'Special Announcement', a broadcast began.

My first impulse was to make for the Radio Centre, but I had no night pass. It turned out that no one was asked to show passes that night. Then I was afraid I should be too late. After all, Radio Centre is some way from us. I couldn't know that the broadcast was to go on till 3 a.m.

But sitting at home I wrote down practically everything that was said.

Shirkov (a worker) said:

'I know that at this moment no one is asleep.' He was right. Who could be asleep at such a time?

Olga Bergholz:

'In January last year we were burying our comrades in the frozen earth, burying them without military honours, naked and in common graves. Instead of a farewell address we gave them an oath—"The Blockade will be broken, we shall win."'

Woman worker Mukhina:

'I came straight from a meeting in our workshop—or rather from meetings in our factory workshops. It's impossible to tell you what it was like, comrades. There are no words. We shall work even harder. Already we have built firing points for which we have received the highest Government award.'

An engineer of X Works, Sokolov:

'Now, at this very moment, while I'm speaking to you, our locksmiths are assembling new fighting units. Long may he live—with whose name on our lips we fight and work and win —our Stalin!'

Ilya Alexandrovich Grusdev:

'Comrades, fellow citizens, fellow countrymen! The thousand times cursed enemy has at last felt the mighty power of the Soviet Army, the mighty power of the Soviet people. We raise the toast to Lenin, the greatest strategist in history, and to Stalin, the heir to Lenin's genius.'

Yerlykin, airman:

'The Fascists were about to strike medals for their soldiers, "For the taking of Leningrad"! They stormed our city many times in their Junkers and Messerschmitts. But the Leningrad sky was, is, and will be a Soviet sky. Long live the man who is now first in our thoughts—Comrade Stalin!'

Tsvetkov, a soldier:

'Let me report how soldiers of my company broke through the Leningrad Blockade.

'Two days ago we attacked the workers' settlement. Our tanks went in against the enemy, and we moved our battalions behind. As we rushed forward, we shouted, "For Comrade Stalin!" "For the city of Lenin!" We dislodged the Fascists, cursed reptiles, from a well-fortified place where every building had been made into a fortress. During the attack I was wounded in the head by an enemy bullet, and blood was streaming down my face. The Commander ordered me to go to the first-aid post. "Comrade Commander," I said, "let me stay until the execution of the set fighting task."

'On the morning of January 17th the settlement was taken by us, and then I went to the field hospital. I have been wounded three times in battles for the city of Lenin. Three times I have shed my blood so that things should be lighter for you. I'm ready to give all my blood, drop by drop, for our final victory.'

Worker of X factory, Tanya Serova:

'What a joyful night it is today! We have been waiting for so long, and now at last we have lived to see it! The black noose with which the enemy tried to strangle our city has been cut. Comrades, we, as well, are participants in the great offensive. For ten days and ten nights the workers in our factory have gone without sleep and respite, to assemble fighting machines for you. These machines went to the Front—for victory!'

All these speeches were interspersed with poems and with songs.

I wrote an essay for foreign circulation, 'They have United'. In its second half I wrote:

'Even during the worst hours of the night, with air raids and shelling, the night shifts carried on in all Leningrad's works. In one printing works alone, in one night, there were forty-seven cases of people wounded by falling lights, torn-out windows, doors and falling plaster.

'During the week preceding the breakthrough of the Blockade, Leningrad carried on in the same way as it had done for the last sixteen months. On this night two concerts were given— Tchaikovsky and Scriabin were performed. In the "Red Army House" they were doing *Russian People* by Simonov. In the Musical Comedy Theatre there was a play, *The Sea Spreads Wide,* featuring the lives of Baltic seamen. In the cinemas there were many Soviet films and two from America. On the 14th January we read in the *Leningrad Pravda* that in the first half of our school year sixty per cent of our children worked well enough to receive "good" and "excellent" for their marks. Though recently one small boy explained to me that he received "unsatisfactory" for arithmetic, "because of an incendiary bomb".

'The other day a fourth-form girl from the 49th School gave a talk to other children on the radio, called "Pigeon, a Military Photographer". And Vova Kisilev from the 52nd School spoke about the training of a first-aid dog.

'On the 17th of January a girl of seven, Lyalya Pritvits, told her mother, a teacher of English, that tomorrow, or the day after, the Blockade would be broken without fail, that her kindergarten had been told this by the army unit with whom they maintain a friendly correspondence. "They will break through the Blockade and bring us some ginger biscuits," Lyalya told her mother.

'And when in the evening of the 18th January the radio announced, "The Blockade is broken", Lyalya jumped out of her little bed. She wore only a nightgown and was shivering with cold and excitement—pale Leningrad child who had survived the Blockade. In order to seem a little taller, she jumped on a chair, and in a loud voice she read a poem she had learned that day in her kindergarten—"Hitler will not escape retribution!"

'This snow-showered moonlight night from the 17th to the 18th of January will never be forgotten by those who lived through it. All of us, in some degree, be we young or old, still have pleasures and sorrows in life ahead of us. The happiness of complete destruction of Nazi Germany, complete liberation from our enemies, is ahead of us, but this joy—the joy of liberated Leningrad—that we shall never forget.

'"They have joined together." This short sentence is heard everywhere: in factories, at H.Q. air defence, in private flats, streets, maternity homes, hospitals, where wounded are lying—the whole of the city.

'It means that the troops of the Leningrad front have joined with the troops of the Volkhov front moving towards Leningrad. It means that the ring of the Blockade has been broken.'*

20th January, 1943. About ten in the evening

The first alert after the breakthrough of the Blockade.

23rd January, 1943

We are increasing the tightening of the encirclement of Stalingrad. On the 8th January, Rokossovsky presented the German 6th Army with an ultimatum. It said, 'A severe Russian winter is only beginning. Hard frosts, cold winds are still ahead. Your position is hopeless.'

The Germans turned down the ultimatum and on the 10th January our general attack began. This is continuing till now. . . .

There is no way out for the Germans at Stalingrad.

24th January, 1943

Am having a series of small (one must hope) reverses. I'm working very badly. I couldn't write anything significant about the breakthrough. I have noticed for some time that I'm rarely successful over solemn occasions. (Switched off the radio for about ten minutes. Have just switched it on again. The metronome is already clicking fast—an alert.)

Things are going to be difficult here. The Germans, like hornets in a hollow tree, fly out and sting. Yesterday we had an

* End of the quote of the article written for foreign circulation.

alert which went on almost all night. One bomb hit the Botanical Gardens again—in the pond. Two others hit the Pionerskaya and Vedenskaya Streets. This will go on again and again. The Germans are avenging themselves for their failure on the fronts, particularly in the northern Caucasus, where we have already taken Armavir.

Outside the cold is ferocious and it isn't warm in our room either. In connection with it, as one of our soldiers said, 'an increased appetite develops'.

26th January, 1943

Just listened to the broadcast of my song 'Hillock X'. The music is pleasant.

27th January, 1943

Yesterday twenty-eight German planes were shot down near the city. Thanks to that, I shall be able to work in peace today. I must make an effort to do something for the 'Tass Window'.

The radio has broken down again, so I don't know what is happening. Efrosiniya Ivanovna said, 'Without the radio we live as if in a dark bottle.'

Bulatov said about the fire on the Bolshoi Prospekt, caused by incendiary bombs: 'meaningful fire'.

28th January, 1943

The liquidation of the 6th German Army at Stalingrad is practically over.

31st January, 1943

A story about the Party Secretary of the Public Library, last winter.

F. and another library worker went to a flat, where, according to their information, a little girl was said to be left.

In the flat it was dead and cold. It had the dreadful look of a flat of last year.

F. and her companion were about to leave when all of a sudden it seemed to them that they could hear a faint sound of breathing.

'Someone is alive here,' said F., and approached the bed which was covered with rags. 'I'll hold the torch and you have a look,' F. said to her companion.

'No,' he replied, 'it's better if I hold it and you have a look.'
Both of them were afraid.

But F. braved it. She threw back the tangled ice-cold blanket. An old man and an old woman were lying in the bed—both dead. In between them a pair of bright eyes shone from the pillow. It was their grandchild, a little girl of three or four years old.

F. took her home. She was covered with bed sores and lice. When she was washed she said:

'Give some porridge.'

She was fed and taken to hospital where everything possible was done for her, but she died seventeen days later. Not even her name was fully established—Mashenka, or perhaps Ninotchka. In her diary, F. calls her 'Ninochka-Mashenka'.

1st February, 1943. Five o'clock in the evening

Went for a little walk. Decided to go my favourite way, by the Botanical Gardens. The Ladoga lorries have left, and the way is now free. However, I had hardly time to reach the main entrance to the gardens when the shelling began. It was as concentrated and as sharp as it was last year in the Sitnoy Market.

There was only a woman with a child in the street with me. She lay down on the pavement, covering the little girl with her body. I ran back home, across the little Karpovka Bridge.

I felt as if I were running towards the gun-fire. But I couldn't stop. I rushed into our courtyard, and straight into our dispensary, which is the nearest building.

And I.D. happened to be there—he had come to get some codeine. When I saw him all my fears vanished at once, and we went home together.

There weren't more than about ten shells. Evidently the gun had been brought up closer, on an ice-yacht.

4th February, 1943

The 6th German Army at Stalingrad has ceased to exist. The communiqué was worded as in the time of the despatches of Peter the Great.

'Taken prisoner: General Field Marshal—1 (Paulus).

'Full Generals—2.

'The remaining—Lt. Generals and Major Generals.'

'Altogether taken prisoner—24 Generals. Total number of prisoners of war—91,000.'

'Fighting in Stalingrad and in the district of Stalingrad is discontinued.'

5th February, 1943

From a letter:

'The people of Leningrad paved the way to the defence of our cities. This was completed by the people of Stalingrad, who have opened a new stage—the crushing of Hitlerite Germany.

'Thank you, Leningraders, for a great service to the whole of mankind and first and foremost to our Soviet people.'

8th February, 1943

I am tormented by neuralgia. Before this started I was 'out of hand', as sometimes one gets 'out of step'.

I don't know what will happen about the journey to Moscow.

9th February, 1943. A clear frosty morning

They started shelling our district at dawn and this went on for about four hours. The bursts varied—sometimes from the air, double, possibly jet propelled, sometimes low, shaking the ground. Shells, in the early morning in a sleeping city, reverberate as if in an empty amphitheatre, where the echo also comes in layers.

Efrosiniya Ivanovna says that the wounded were brought in 'wearing their clothes, and pouring with blood'. One shell burst outside the Mosque.

This is the way the Germans are avenging themselves for everything—Stalingrad, in the first instance, Kursk, and Karocha which they lost yesterday.

10th February, 1943

I feel like nothing on earth. I couldn't keep to my schedule. I have lost my 'rhythm', which for me is a real catastrophe. I can't achieve anything in fits and starts, only with an unhurried but uninterrupted effort.

Neuralgia has got the better of me, and I'm driven mad by the hopelessness of the telephone. All my arrangements are being frustrated. The journey to Moscow is suspended in mid-air. So far as a prose book is concerned, I shall have to write it in quite a different way from what I thought.

The worst thing at such a time is that my will is getting weaker. The 'will muscle' has just got slack. You know what you have to do, and you haven't the strength to do it. The bow can't shoot, the bow-string has got weak.

What I must do today:

1. Even though I feel so weak, in no circumstances to lie down. To go down, ensconce myself at that telephone, and make all my arrangements.

2. To finish the 'Tass Window' (I had begun it at dawn).

3. To complain less. Complaining uses up a great deal of energy.

About literary 'placing'. Mere feeling by itself is so volatile both in verse and in prose. One must have solid, concrete details in writing. This is the best 'stabiliser'.

11th February, 1943

My illness may be for the good, for the reason that it can serve as a watershed between verse and prose. I think all the time about a book in prose. The journey to Moscow is still in the air. (Another alert. I can't remember how many we've had.)

We are beating the Germans—already we are near Kharkov. About the state of confusion in Germany, 'I'm reading and cannot read enough', as Pushkin said. It's true, of another occasion.

12th February, 1943

Outside—an uncomfortable thaw. This is not like the winter of last year, with its 'grim tenderness'. At present everything is thawing, it is a dirty, slippery evening. Neuralgia has taken me over, it tortures me as mice would love to torture a cat.

In such weather it's good to bury oneself in work. The journey to Moscow is being postponed. The airfields have become sodden, and as yet there is no direct rail link. In a word, however you may try to avoid it, you have to get down to work.

14th February, 1943. About eight o'clock in the evening

A barrage of shelling during dinner. The whole building felt the strength of the blows, it gasped as if it had been winded. I was torn between two desires—a longing for tea, and a longing to go down from the third floor. I gulped my tea, standing up, scalding myself, it was so hot, but I simply couldn't tear myself away from it.

When at last we went down to H.Q. everything grew quiet. So far it is still quiet, but how will it be tonight? The moon is at its brightest.

15th February, 1943

My dream: on a whole page of newspaper—a new type of swallow with a propeller, and its area of distribution—a whole enormous continent. I think this is how a little boy was reflected in my dream. He was charming and serious, in long ski pants and rabbit fur hat. The boy was walking with his grand-mother and looking into the sky, to see whether German planes were flying. The mother was walking away. As she waved her hand, she said:

'Don't be afraid, Vovik, don't be afraid. Your granny is with you.'

A powerful protection indeed!

We have taken Rostov and Voroshilovgrad.

In the evening

Merciless moon. True, there is no alert, but the shelling goes on. Very heavy gun-fire. There are no lights anywhere in the city. Evidently some main cable has been damaged. A small paraffin lamp is burning in our place; it has to be refilled very often.

Marietta is preparing for her lecture tomorrow: 'Prussic Acid', and something else. I.D. is trying in vain to get some-one on the telephone.

A kind of tiredness in everything.

No, Leningrad's difficulties aren't over yet. And this break-through of the Blockade isn't final, either. No, the Leningrad epic can't end like that. Everything will be different, more frightening, on a grander scale.

15th February, 1943

Little by little I am being drawn back into a working routine. I repeat to myself for the thousandth time that one cannot 'give up one's schedule'.

To work without stopping—this is vital.

25th February, 1943

On the eve of the Red Army Day, at the request of the anti-aircraft battery crews, I.D. and I spoke at one of the gun-sites. I.D. gave a report on the international situation, I gave a reading. The battery is stationed at the Tuchkov Bridge, on some barges moored to the bank.

We were taken there, past the Lenin Stadium, along wooden gangways. The Neva is still ice-bound, so cold it seems that no spring will ever be able to battle its way through.

On deck girl A.A. gunners were at their guns under a gloomy evening sky.

We spoke below, in a cabin so small you couldn't swing a cat.* Before I read the Commander took the floor. He said:

'You, Comrade Inber, hear the voice of our guns practically every evening, and now we are going to listen to yours. Usually we can only hear you on the radio.'

5th March, 1943

A most interesting essay by Danchenko in the *Leningrad Pravda* —'A Workshop of Artificial Albumin'—about protein yeast. The factory began working a year ago, during the worst days of the Blockade. Professor Sharkov, assistant lecturer Kaly-uzhny, engineer Iztik, designer Petrova, senior chemist Zborodova, chief technological expert Sartanya and others worked there.

'Amongst thousands of different species a bacteria of the yeast fungus was found—a minute chemical machine, producing albumin in its body from the sugary substance of pulp. . . .'

The factory was built right on the front line.

'At night, installation crews, the builders of the project and its future users, travelled to the advance defence lines. There in no-man's-land, in a building riddled with shells, stood machines without which the work could not start. They were taken apart some 100 metres from the enemy dugouts. Infinite care had to be taken so that a frozen hand should not shake, a treacherous clink of metal ring out. At dawn the men returned, dragging their heavy loads.'

* The expression used in Russian: 'Not only an apple couldn't fall, but there would be no place for a nut.'

A description of the process of production followed.

'The first samples were taken. A quaint changing world is visible in the microscope lenses. Vague shadows rush by like arrows—these are the mortal enemies and rivals of the yeast fungus. They are devouring food intended for it, they hunt it down.

'A whole staff of chemists helps the fungus in its desperate struggle for existence. This drama unrolls itself on the surface of the tank, calm enough in its outward appearance. The temperature is checked every second, and the composition of the culture medium. Outlines of the yeast fungus, looking like coffee beans, come into view, getting increasingly sharper. The high temperature, having spared them, has destroyed their enemies.

'The concentration of sugar rises. New litres of must rush into the tank. The "coffee beans" come to life, waking from their former stupor. They have adapted themselves to their surroundings and take their "food" eagerly.

'Three more hours. Greyish-brown foam sweeps over the brim of the tank. The fungii increase by half a ton. The yield is fivefold.

'Some more time goes by, and then the separators go into action. "Powerful centrifuges separate the water." Then, at last, "a light brown plastic mass appears. It is albumin yeast, a kilogram of which replaces three kilograms of meat." '

I read this, being unable to tear myself away from it. Now I shall look on yeast products, which we eat so often, with different eyes.

10th March, 1943. Moscow

As we didn't want to wait for the plane any longer, we went by train. We had a difficult journey, with raids both in the air and on the ground.

There is as yet no direct passenger connection between Leningrad and Moscow. Only cargo trains go straight across a pontoon bridge near Schlisselburg, where the Neva leaves the Ladoga. Railwaymen call this bridge the 'Corridor of Death'. It is shot right through by the Germans. Everything with which we are supplied, every sack of flour, every tin, goes through this 'Corridor'. I remembered the story of a seaman from Ladoga, of how he was carrying a valuable cargo to Leningrad in his motor launch. It was before the break-through of the

Blockade. Bombing started; all the boat crew were wounded, but the helmsman could still steer. 'And did you bring everything in all right?' I asked. 'What kind of cargo was it?' The seaman answered: 'Cocoa and chocolate for Leningrad's children.'

I.D. and I boarded the train at the Finnish station. It was chock full. We arrived at Borisova Griva late in the evening. It was pitch dark. We found the head of the evacuation centre, and pulled our suitcases on sleighs in the wet snow, to the centre, where we spent the night.

The beds smelled of disinfectant, but were immaculately clean. We lit the stove and got some food. A lantern had been left for us. In the morning, an ambulance, going to the other side of Ladoga, took us to Kabony—birthplace of Alexander Prokofiev. The spring thaw had already started, and the car went through puddles.

In Kabony, as we were boarding the train, there was an alert. It caught up with us for the second time in the evening, in Volkhov where a lot of convoys had gathered. As machine-guns fired from the planes, I asked I.D.—shouldn't I get up (I was lying in an upper bunk). He answered:

'And where will you go?'

And indeed there was nowhere to go. To right and left—trains, and further on, a bombed-out station, then wasteland, ruins . . . so we stayed in our bunks.

25th March, 1943

Among all my Muscovite affairs I am thinking all the time about the 'Spring' part of the 'Pulkovsky'. I would like to present the spring in Leningrad as the winter was presented in Part Two.

27th March, 1943

A story from engineer P. about one of our defence factories. The factory split into two parts—the cadet branch left its parent and moved to the Urals. There, with extraordinary speed, it rebuilt its workshops, and began to work successfully. It captured from it venerable parent the coveted Challenge Red Banner, and to add insult to injury, sent a letter of consolation to its parent.

14th April, 1943

Not for a long time has an arrival given so much pleasure as the return to Leningrad.

This time Moscow was endlessly frustrating for me. After the telephone orgies, an enormous amount of small and minutely detailed business arrangements, after the unbearable feeling of 'Oh Lord, I'm not coping, I'm late', after sad letters from Jeanne, and the final *débâcle*, when we arrived too late at the airport and had to come back to the hotel, and I clenched my teeth and unpacked and packed our things again—after all this, came a marvellous journey. It wasn't tiring. The only bad thing was that I froze on the plane. It was terribly cold. A dry, clear cold day of early spring.

We landed at Khvoinaya *en route*. Sunset, cloudless sky. A crescent moon—brilliant, looking like some part of a plane, maybe aluminium, maybe silver. A seat became free at Khvoinaya, and I sat in it. How pleasant it was after a hard bench. I settled comfortably, leaned back against some matrices of *Pravda,* I believe, and slept although I was frozen all over. I saw Ladoga as in a dream. The centre of it was already free of ice. Everything was quiet. We flew without an escort.

We entered a spellbound city. The moon was out. There was an alert on. A light soundless night. The trams had stopped, the empty streets were in a cold, moonlit mist of spring. It's all so different from Moscow!

And now a special coach took passengers up to the Liteiny Prospekt, which is very convenient.

And the houses, how they all shine and smell with cleanliness. The night was silent, no Germans disturbed us. Having been frozen on the plane, I fell fast asleep now. And this one Leningrad night washed off me all the tiredness of those long Moscow days.

Really, Leningrad is so calm after Moscow, so well suited to work.

This morning I decided that no matter how hard it will be, I must try and do something with Part Five. I may be able to reshape it or I may have to start afresh.

I would like to write about the Baltic Fleet, about the tragedy of the warship that is still unable to sail. There is nowhere for her to go, it's as if she had put down roots in the water. She is a mighty battleship, a sea eagle, yet she must envy the 'small sea birds'—the lesser craft, torpedo boats, corvettes. (A loud burst of gun-fire, and I can hear the birds twittering. They have got used to it all and are not afraid.) One could write a song of a ship, full of romanticism, of anger, pent-up fury: 'Where are the seas on which I sailed?'

It is going to be a war spring in 1943. The war is still going on, the end isn't in sight yet. (Again everything is quiet, the guns can't be heard any longer.)

16th April, 1943

Marietta and I went for a walk, and we had to come back because we were being heavily shelled. Shrapnel was falling all around. We thought of going on, but we met Efrosiniya Ivanovna, who told us:

'They are falling everywhere, everywhere. One just exploded at the smithy, and I crawled here . . .'

And the smithy is just next door to the dispensary where we were going. It's a marvellous day, a spring wind, but not too strong. 'It's good to be alive on such a day', as Jimmy Collins, the American airman, said. Since then he has died.

Yesterday, Tikhonov, Vishnevsky, Kron, Azarov, Bergholz and Makogonenko came to see me. I 'reported' to them about Moscow. It was gay and enjoyable. They left for their homes during an alert. People say that there was strong shelling in the night, but I never even woke up.

What a pity it would be to die now, when one wants so much to live! I shall never be able to forget Leningrad and all its facets. If only I stay alive, I mean to write a great deal more about it.

17th April, 1943

Horrible night! Horrible moonlit night! Raids began early, and anti-aircraft guns were firing throughout the city. Later, it got somewhat quieter and we fell asleep . . . we woke up again because of vibration . . . not because of noise. The bed began to shake. I remember it was just like that a long time ago, during the earthquake in the Crimea, and even earlier, in Odessa, when I was a little girl. It was a strong underground shock, then. It happened at night, in the summer, and I, clad only in a nightgown, ran barefoot through the flat to my father.

Seven o'clock

Returned from a walk. Immediately behind our buildings Leo Tolstoy Street is blocked off. There is a notice which says: 'Danger. Drivers and pedestrians are forbidden to go through here'. An unexploded bomb is lying nearby. It fell in the passage we usually take to go to the District Committee. It will be defused.

Tonight, of course, the same is in store for us.

18th April, 1943. Five o'clock in the evening

Just came back from town. Have been to the Olympiad of Children's Art, organised by the Pioneers' Palace jointly with the Institute of Advanced Teachers' Training. The Olympiad has already been opened for a few days, and schools from all districts are taking part in it—that is to say those schools that haven't been evacuated.

In the halls of the 'Palace' children simultaneously sing, dance, recite, take part in an orchestra. The rooms have been cleaned and heated as far as possible. An exhibition of drawings, handiwork and clay modelling has been organised.

In a small blue hall under a dome, the 341st School of the Volodarsky District performed the song 'Makhorochka' with its own orchestra. For the convenience of the public, some of the performers sat on chairs. Those who stood treated those who sat with open contempt.

One of the performers was in the throes of losing his front milk teeth. He was temporarily transferred to conducting, so that he could stand with his back to the audience.

Vitya Ivanov, who laughs easily, was playing the accordion. He was constantly hiding his face behind the instrument. On his jacket he wore the stripes of a corporal of a summer unit.

The 116th School of the Vyborg District showed a puppet theatre *Clever Petrushka*. The cast—Punch, a girl swineherd, a horse and a cow.

Older schoolgirls recited poetry. The stern and bitter words of the stanzas of Bergholz and my 'Pulkovsky Meridian' sounded very different on children's lips.

In conclusion we watched some Russian dances. A year ago these children couldn't dance—they could walk only with difficulty, because they were so weak.

L.D.—K

From the Children's Palace we went to the Kazan Cathedral to visit the grave of Kutuzov. We had been planning to do this for a long time.

April clouds gathered over the Nevsky. It was chilly and windy.

In the cathedral—marble cold. A slanting shaft of sunlight looked as if it were smoking between the columns. Banners are lowered over the tomb. On a memorial tablet engraved in gold are the words of Suvorov about Kutuzov at the Assault of Ismail: 'He was at my left flank, but was my right hand'.

Returned home. Four shells have fallen in our grounds during our absence.

19th April, 1943

Admirable non-flying weather: cloudy, raining. If only such weather put the artillery off, as well!

27th April, 1943

Caught a cold in the Philharmonic Hall, at a concert given in memory of Rachmaninov. These large stone buildings gather in the winter cold and keep it there until the next winter.

The hall was full. I recognised many people whom I used to see there, when we sat in our felt boots and fur coats. Things are different now. In those days the chandeliers burnt with a quarter of their power, and now the crystal pendants blaze with light. Many servicemen were wearing decorations which didn't exist in the autumn of 1941.

Only it was so cold.

I sat and felt I was becoming ill. But I hadn't the strength to tear myself away from the Second Concerto (piano with orchestra). This work has a magical effect on me ... I can't find words. It makes me tremble* ... this cold, combined with the cold of the hall, and two hard frosts have made me catch a chill. And now I'm really down with it.

29th April, 1943. Noon

Yesterday's shelling was one of the heaviest, if not the heaviest, of the whole time of the Blockade. Two hundred and twenty shells fell, but not on us. They fell in the Kuibyshev District.

* In Russian: 'frost goes over my skin'.

We only heard the rumblings from afar but they were so loud, they seemed to be in our part of the city.

A shell hit the H.Q. of the City Air Defence Centre and killed the Commissar. A shell pierced the Radio Centre Building right through, destroying the studio where the 'latest radio news' is broadcast. What a good thing all the staff had been ordered down to the shelter!

And again we hear even more of this persistent rumour of an assault on the city. In the square near the offices of the *Leningrad Pravda* pill-boxes of unprecedented strength are being built.

My right ear hurts me. There is a weakness, and noises. But my morale is high and I'm pleased with my article about children, and with my verses.

1st May, 1943. *About noon*

Woke at nine because the house was swaying. It swayed and rocked like a swing. This was Hitler's way of 'congratulating' us on May 1st. There weren't many shells, about eight fired one after another, evidently from an armoured platform. A second such 'barrage' took place in the afternoon, but this one wasn't so bad.

A charming concert was broadcast last night at half past twelve. Hawaiian guitars and old-fashioned songs sounded touching on the air which had so recently reverberated with gun-fire.

9th May, 1943

At last I have got back to my equilibrium, after being ill for a fortnight. I began to develop pneumonia but was given 'Sulphidin'. This called off the pneumococci, but it nearly finished me as well.

Now it's all over, but the neuralgia is still in my head. Yesterday I had an attack of it that lasted six hours.

And what a magnificent spring started while I was battling with the pneumococci. Even lying by the window I can look out at the tender young leaves. An orgy of making allotments has seized the city. And here I lie. I have done absolutely nothing this year.

10th May, 1943

Today my head feels worse again, and altogether I am weak, pale and poisoned by drugs. I clutch a hot-water bottle wrapped in a woollen cover. Awful!

At last the window in the big room has been opened . . . and the spring air is pouring through it like a breath of paradise!

I lay awake all night because of an unbearable inner anxiety. All the plans I haven't carried out, all the intentions I haven't fulfilled, the letters not written, the telegrams not sent, the stanzas insufficiently thought out—all this whirled round me like a terrifying wheel, the unfortunate axle of which was myself. I lit the light and worked for a bit on some rough stanzas for a future poem. After that I felt better and fell asleep.

13th May, 1943. In the afternoon

The alert is over. It was one of the longest. Marietta and I were in the courtyard at the very moment the Germans flew over us. The anti-aircraft guns roared, the sky was filled with dark puffs of smoke. As an airman who came from the Front said: 'The Fritzes are trying to carry out a mass raid.' Then he added that they have brought up new reinforcements, but Leningrad 'won't have to suffer for long'.

The weather deteriorated again, but sometimes the evenings are extraordinarily golden, tinged dusky light blue, with a small but dazzlingly bright crescent moon, and stars as big as planets.

22nd May, 1943

I am waiting to be taken to the Kirov works. They have been asking me to come and speak there for ages, but I was always ill or busy . . . I hear a hoot under the windows—that's for me.

Evening

Just returned from the Kirovsky. There was a very large audience. They listened well, although I read very badly since my illness. I was short of breath all the time.

The factory club is in the air-raid shelter. The Germans, after all, are right next door.

It's impossible to look at this place without excitement. It is almost Stalingrad, as described in Vassily Grossman's article 'The Direction of the Main Thrust'.

Here, as well, 'are the dark bulk of the workshops, rails palely wet and shining, already touched here and there with oxydisation. A pile-up of smashed goods trucks, of coal, gaunt factory chimneys, pierced in many places by German shells.'

But in contrast with Stalingrad the 'main thrust' against the Kirov works is split into many ceaseless attacks.

When we came out of the basement shelter, into the fresh air, we were met by the sounds of a waltz. The gramophone stood in the open, on a fragment of brick, and two pairs of girls of the fire-fighting squad, wearing trousers and canvas boots, were slowly circling the yard against a background of a burned-out workshop. Overhead—as if it were protecting them in their short hour of gaiety—a fighter 'Hawk' plane was patrolling.

I remembered the factory 'Sevkabel'* on Vassilievsky Island, where I went last summer. The Germans hit the 'Sevkabel' from the opposite side of the gulf, from Ligovo. There, too, all the workshops had been badly damaged. A flowering bush looked daringly from the courtyard through a gaping hole in one of the buildings.

Leningrad is surrounded by these great works, like 'Sentinels', as in the old days it was surrounded by 'watch-tower' monasteries.

24th May, 1943

Yesterday I went to give a talk to a naval unit, stationed, however, inland behind the Spasskaya post, in a small place called Medvezhy Stan. The river Okhta flows near. Everything is smothered in bird-cherry blossom.

In the car I was snowed under with great bouquets of it, and the sentry, when he was checking my pass, said:

'And where is the Citizen herself?'

I gave everyone in our corridor great bunches of blossom.

25th May, 1943. 3.10

Just now there was a mighty sound like a great crack in the air that I nearly fell off my chair. I'd never heard anything like it

* Northern Cable Works.

before. Then seconds later the crack was repeated. I thought it was a bomb, but it was more likely shrapnel.

Efrosiniya Ivanovna was just about to wash a window, but she said:

'That's completely spoiled my mood.'

And she didn't go on with the washing.

A third crack, and the radio is silent.

Later

Bulatov has put my mind at rest. He says it's us, some new kind of 'toy' placed somewhere near and tested.

26th May, 1943

Professor Abramson, a very gifted surgeon, and lecturer at our Institute, was killed yesterday by a shell. A few days ago he visited Marietta (I heard his voice through the wall) and asked if he might show me some poems written by his little girl. Marietta answered that I was busy at present, and that it would be better to wait for a few days.

At the time of his death Abramson was expected at a meeting of the Scientific Council of the Blood Transfusion Institute. He finished his lecture to the students at the Karl Marx Hospital twenty minutes early, so as not to be late. He was a punctual man and used to say about himself, 'I am never late.'

27th May, 1943

Abramson was killed by a bomb splinter, not by a shell. Half his head was torn off. Marietta saw him yesterday, in his coffin. The head was hidden by a gauze bandage, the empty space being filled with cotton wool.

His old parents are here in Leningrad.

28th May, 1943

Mariya Nikolayevna Egerstrem, of the Institute of Advanced Training of Teachers, came to see me yesterday.

The windows in Mariya Nikolayevna's flat were blown out five times by bomb blast. After the sixth time it became impossible to live there any longer, and M.N. got a new flat in exchange for her battered old place. But how was she to move her belongings when nine kilos of bread have been asked for the piano alone?

When they learned about this, colleagues of Mariya Nikolayevna organised a 'working Saturday' for moving her furniture and other possessions. The move lasted for three days, and everything was carried by hand, with the exception of the piano. All the moving was done by women. Amongst other things there was a heavy bronze lamp of Prometheus, holding a torch aloft.

When she had settled down in her new home Mariya Nikolayevna arranged a house-warming, spending her blood donor's extra ration on refreshments.

There was tea, sandwiches and salad. The guests were all given presents. Each one had a notice on his plate, giving the right to receive a 'parcel'. These parcels were carefully wrapped and bore the recipient's full address. In each parcel there was something to give special pleasure to the addressee. An expert on Pushkin received a small bust of Pushkin, a lover of porcelain, a small antique plate. Those who had children— children's books.

The house-warming was very successful, despite the usual raid. Guests drank tea and chatted. Over them, Prometheus brandished his torch: the light is working in the new flat.

Mariya Nikolayevna came to me with a request that I sit on the jury of a children's literary competition. She brought me a great number of papers, exercise books, verses, stories, diaries, scientific essays—there were the most divergent subjects.

A pupil in the fourth form of the 26th School describes the invasion of German troops into Russian towns:

> 'They were marching into towns
> Looting shops without distinction,
> Drinking vodka, taking fat,
> Smashing tins and gulping quickly.'

And a 'maturer' sixth-form pupil sent in a research essay, 'The Book is the Friend of Man'. We learned from it that 'during the eighteenth to the twentieth centuries mankind made considerable progress in its development'.

There were genuinely valuable things such as, for instance, 'Fatherland War in memoires of Leningrad school-children' (sixth form, 10th School).

The story, 'The First Bomb' by Pioneer* girl Zina Karaseva, was interesting.

'Night. Quiet. Stars. The moon shines brightly on the streets. I am lying on the roof, by the chimney, listening intently in the silence, and I look up into the sky. There is the Great Bear, there the Small. To my great surprise, a new star appears, next to the Great Bear. Suddenly there is the drone of an engine—clearer, and clearer. I realised it was an enemy plane.' Further on, Zina describes the drone, the crashes, the sound of falling glass. 'From below they are shouting, "Zina, Zina!..." I run down. My parents, who hadn't expected to see me alive, can't believe their eyes. But I, paying no attention to this, ask, "What did the Bomb hit?" And I am told it has hit the house next to ours. So I rush there to help carry out the casualties and dress their wounds.'

A ninth-form pupil of the 47th School, Inna Bityugova, wrote an essay somewhat drearily called 'What Work on a State farm has given me'. But in fact it was full of charm and poetry. Inna writes that even before the war she was 'dreaming of doing something good and useful. So that I might not have lived in vain.'

'A new, absorbing interest in growing things began' for Leningrad school-children in the summer of 1942. 'We started allotments and it became a time of rewarding labour. Gradually, the life of plants absorbed me. It seemed to me that I was cultivating minute people. Here they were, barely visible, but already their little legs were getting stronger, their little green heads were proudly raised. And as I looked at them, I realised that an old dream of mine had come true.

'I imagined two roads—one leading to the Front, the other to my city. And along these roads small green vegetable dwarfs ran, one after the other. One of them ran up to a large stone house. On a bed in one of the flats, a little fair girl sat; her arms were as thin as sticks, her cheeks were hollow, her eyes were sad. Her enemies had brought hunger to her. But my green dwarf was more powerful than all the enemy armies put together. He had come to help the little weak girl. Now, her cheeks are growing rosy, her arms round, her eyes shine again. She gets up and walks, and I feel that in her, my dream has come true.

'Another little vegetable man ran along the second road. He

* Member of a Child Communist Organisation—children of school age.

was surrounded by enemies who tried not to let him through. They dropped bombs and fired shells but he was invincible. He ran into a dugout, where a soldier-scout sat, bent over a map. He had a long march ahead of him. Suddenly he realised: he is no longer lonely, Soviet children were thinking of him and caring for him. The soldier ate the vegetable and felt a giant's strength pour into his veins. Courageously, he marched on to victory. And soon, the Soviet flag is hoisted over the Soviet land. . . .'

Bityugova completes the story thus:

'I know now what hard work means, and I feel responsible for the work I do. I feel I'm not a child schoolgirl any more, but a schoolgirl warrior. I have worked for the city and for the Front.'

On the cover of Inna Bityugova's story a beetroot, a turnip and small radishes are depicted in colour, all with little friendly faces.

Verses by Vorozheikina are good.

3rd June, 1943

It's a hot day, quite like summer, I went with Anna Ivanovna to fetch our hats, and heard an alert. Our tram stopped at the Marsovo Pole, and we all sheltered under a gateway. We could see the blue arc of the sky as if it were at the end of a tunnel. It was cloudless and brilliant.

A few minutes ago there had been another broadcast about the sale of anti-mustard gas paste No. 5 in unlimited quantities.

4th June, 1943

Efrosiniya Ivanovna informed me that the 'Germans have flooded us with leaflets'. Once again, there is gun-fire. Just now, this very moment somewhere close, there was a noise that wasn't a bang—more like a hiss.

Well, I shall embark on what I call the 'Pushkin' poem.

We shall be speaking on the radio on the 144th anniversary of Pushkin's death at his flat on the Moika.

7th June, 1943

The new Part Five is ready in the form of 'dough for the oven'. It's only necessary to see that it doesn't turn sour. Old Man Goethe warned us on that score a long time ago.

Yesterday we gave a reading in Pushkin's flat. I had never been there before. The rooms are bare, as everything was taken away and hidden at the beginning of the Blockade. On the chimney-piece and window-sills there are bouquets of bird-cherry blossom and of lilac. (The lilac this year is fantastic—wonderful heavy sprays, they might be carved in marble.) And a delicate scent of slightly faded flowers followed us from room to room. A microphone was fixed in Pushkin's study, next to the empty shelves. The house is well preserved, the floors polished, but cracks are spreading everywhere. The walls in Pushkin's former bedroom are in a particularly bad condition.

In the courtyard, under the very windows of the study—a bomb crater.

I have written a small report for *Pravda* about all this. One should do such things more often. One mustn't ignore journalist in oneself but keep all three writers alive-in-one—the poet, the prose writer, the journalist.

It's a wonderful day—one of the thirty-five cloudless days of Leningrad. There are thirty-five of them in a year. I discovered this in the *Great Soviet Encyclopedia,* in an article on 'Leningrad'.

8th June, 1943

Today at the Smolny I received a medal, 'For the Defence of Leningrad'. There were a few of us in Popkov's study—representatives of art and science. No one of them said anything when we were presented with our medals. For myself, I was much too dumbfounded to utter a word.

This small disc has absorbed everything into it, all Leningrad, and all our memories of it for the rest of our lives.

10th June, 1943

I.D. refuses to eat or drink. I hardly see him at all. His many problems have almost finished him off.

Roosevelt's declaration at a press conference about the possibility of chemical warfare was broadcast. Can it be that this too is in store for us? Everything that the earth has suffered in its millions of years pales before this horror.

I look at the green trees as if I were saying good-bye to them.

Already I see them turned to dust and ashes.

14th June, 1943

I.D. returned today from the 'peat cutting'. Things aren't going too well there; the work is heavy, and the students are having a hard time.

15th June, 1943

'Allotment bulletin.' Yuri Vladimirovich Baimakov, doctor of chemistry, who completed the second volume of his work *Electrolysis in Metallurgy,* exhibited a turnip weighing six kilogrammes in the vegetable show at the 'House of Scientists'. In his allotment near the Polytechnic Institute he has also grown potatoes, but he doesn't eat them. He withstood the temptation and left them for the seeds. Now he has planted seed potatoes. He carted the bags of manure himself, and used superphosphate and calcium chloride as fertilisers. The yield from a hundred metres of ground is six hundred kilogrammes of vegetables.

Despite the paper shortage, Baimakov's book is being published.

Vera Radionovna Strechneva, meritorious artist of the Republic, has been on the stage for thirty-nine years. Her allotment is in the courtyard, and the yield is good.

In the Marsovo Pole the professors' allotments stretch from one end to the other. I once saw an old professor sprinkle his cabbage with naphthalene, saving it from a harmful bug.

18th June, 1943

Went with Vasilyeva and a photographer to the island named after Kirov, and now called 'The Children's Island'. In its seventeen buildings and pavilions a Pioneers' Camp is housed, the first of its kind since the Blockade. Nine hundred and forty-two children are here now, but fifteen hundred are going to live here in the future.

When people arrive from the city the first question the children ask is: 'Is there any shelling?' or, 'Which district is being shelled?' One boy asked:

'What is the prognosis for today?'

Another, aged fourteen, begged us to get him taken back to town:

'Mother has a two-month-old baby. I want to go to see how she is managing without me.'

The children are being well fed. They are given glucose and milk.

In an article to be published abroad I wrote:

'In the best district of the city, on the "Islands" ("Ostrova"), luxurious private houses were built before the Revolution. Now they are lived in by children whose fathers are at the Front, and whose mothers work for the defence. All the best premises are given to them. The staff live in what used to be the quarters inhabited by housekeepers, linen maids and butlers in bygone days.

'There was an exception in one such house that has formerly belonged to a wealthy fish merchant. I noticed that a wonderful room with a view over the river Okhta was occupied, not by children, but by their young girl teacher.

'Sensing my unasked question, the young girl blushed to the roots of her hair—up to where a wreath of daisies had been placed on her fair plaits. It happened to be the hour when the children collected "medicinal" herbs, but evidently pure aesthetics were not excluded.

'"Yes, yes, you are right," said the girl, "at least fifteen children could be put in this room, but look . . . look at the ceiling."

'I looked up at the ornate semicircular dome. There, in "decadent" shades of greenish purple, a heavy-breasted naked Eve was depicted in the Garden of Eden. A serpent with a dubious expression on its face was offering her an apple.

'"As a teacher, I couldn't let the children look at that picture," continued the girl with the daisies, "and I found they were doing just that. Those figures frightened the tiny ones and made them cry. We haven't yet got the chalk to whitewash the ceiling. When the Blockade is really lifted, then . . . Meanwhile I sleep in here. The children only come in here when I am forced to reprimand them. But then, you understand, they don't raise their eyes."

'In conclusion, the young teacher added with pleasure that she has to admonish the children more and more frequently, because they have become strong enough to be naughty.

'"When they came they were so weak." '

24th June, 1943. Eleven o'clock in the morning

Heavy shelling, but it's difficult to know exactly where the shells are falling. They fly past with a whistle and burst with a whistle. Evidently it's not in our district, as the radio is broadcasting Sofronitsky. (Oh, a thud nearby . . .)

I am giving a talk on poetry on 3rd July. (It seems to me that it is us, too, firing simultaneously.)

I am depressed about I.D. His problems are forever growing. Peat-cutting, allotments, anti-aircraft defence service, all that in addition to his ordinary work.

(At last the radio has reported shelling.)

25th June, 1943

It's a weight off my mind and I'm slightly less worried for I.D. He revived a little because he has received an adequate consignment of gardening implements for the allotments, also albumen yeast for those engaged in digging peat.

30th June, 1943

That was quite a burst of gun-fire! And near too! Once again shelling is starting. Once again a whistle and a burst.

4th July, 1943

A small event. A kitten. We now have a kitten, the son of Mashka from the main kitchen. We call him Kuzya. He is very thin, and looks like a midget. He is very unsteady on his little legs, and moves crabwise.

Everyone is coming to have a look at Kuzya. Bad rickets in his hindquarters are diagnosed.

Kittens—they are a universal enthusiasm. Everyone wants to have a small, living animal. Apart from anything else, rats are getting the upper hand. I thought up a riddle—'Two thousand, with a small tail—what is it!' The answer is—a kitten. That is what he would be worth, if he were obtained with money. A small dacha on the Lisy Nos was offered in exchange for a grown-up, experienced cat. But this is a district that is much under fire. Whether they found such a cat, I don't know.

6th July, 1943

The Germans have gone over to the offensive at the Orlov, Kursk and Belgorod sectors. Fighting continues. We have damaged several hundreds of tanks (over five hundred) and shot down more than two hundred planes. It is possible that the tide has turned.

7th July, 1943

The Germans have been repulsed in the Orlov sector, but not so far at Belgorod, where things are still very tense.

8th July, 1943

Yesterday the shelling went on at intervals all day. I hear I.D. on the telephone, giving permission to some poor mother to spend the night in the hospital, where her boy is lying with a bad stomach wound.

The night report on the radio was middling—we are still in a tight corner at Belgorod.

12th July, 1943

My birthday went off well. I was genuinely gay (it doesn't happen with me often), having drunk a little vodka. Everyone else was gay, too.

I received some beautiful roses from the editorial offices of the *Leningrad Pravda*. I haven't seen anything like them since the beginning of the war. They are on my table now.

Four o'clock

Two bursts. Terribly near. I hid the typewriter, just in case.

15th July, 1943

I got myself into what I call 'a whirlpool'.

If one visualises life in the form of a river (I remember the wonderful story by Kuprin called 'The River of Life') . . . if one visualises life in the form of a river, down which you swim, not too easily, but steadily enough, then in this river whirlpools of unknown depth happen at times.

Sometimes you manage to struggle against it, you glide along the edge, you are at the end of your tether, but then, at last . . . Hurray! You have succeeded. And, at times, you are sucked, gyrating, down lower and lower until you seem to be lying on the river bed.

Somewhere above you, life flows blessedly on, somewhere your desk is standing, and work you had begun progresses smoothly. Events take place, meetings swim by, and here you are, at the point of no return, exhaustion. Weakness, weakness . . . endless distaste for any kind of action.

And still the only way to get out of the whirlpool is to make the effort by yourself. It's like freezing to death—you want to fall asleep, but you must get up. It is cold, but you must rub yourself with snow. You've got to work. It's what saves you.

And you want so much to lie down and do nothing!

I am tired, my friends, mortally tired! . . .

17th July, 1943

It was impossible to sleep from four in the morning onwards. At first there were A.A. guns, and then a barrage of shelling. Now it's nine o'clock and it's all gradually dying down. Bursts are getting more distant, like a thunderstorm that is moving away.

Yesterday I was on the outskirts of the city, in the Institute's allotments. I paid a visit to Yu. A. Mendeleva.

I saw with a kind of, I would say astonishment, that nature is continuing life as usual. Its creations are as beautiful as ever.

Such lofty reflections were inspired by things we had taken as a matter of course in peace time—a calf, strawberries, roses—and which are now simply shattering.

The calf reminds me of our Kuzya, only bigger—the same long legs, the same unsteady sideways gait.

Strawberries, redcurrants, raspberries—all these are for the production of vitamins for the charges of Yliya Aronovna.

But my poor Part Five reminds me of sour milk which is not allowed to settle. It's beginning to become curds and is covered with a layer of sour cream, when I shake it up yet again. And all is lost.

18th July, 1943

Today is fifty years since the birth of Mayakovsky. I have a lecture to give in the lecture hall, and a talk on the radio. But the German guns are firing so hard in nearly all districts, I'm at a loss as to what I should do. The trams aren't working, the lines have been damaged in so many places. The telephone doesn't work, so that I can't ring the lecture hall and ask if the meeting will take place. And I.D. says I must go without fail, since I am the lecturer. He will, of course, go with me.

We shall take all important documents with us—just in case. It might be a good idea to take the typewriter, too.

It's wiser to take everything with us, otherwise we may get home and find there is no home.

19th July, 1943

The evening in memory of Mayakovsky was an outstanding success. There weren't too many people—about a hundred. We were all transferred to the small hall. But it was indeed touching that people turned up at all to attend a literary evening in such circumstances.

After my introductory words, Tikhonov, Ryvina and some actors carried on.

Later, I spoke on the radio. We went home along quiet streets. (By that time the shelling had entirely ceased.)

A lecture on poetry is looming ahead of me.

24th July, 1943. Evening

Terrifying day! The Germans have acquired a new technique— a great number of short shellings. By this means they are inflicting a lot of casualties, as the first shell is always the most deadly, being unexpected. Besides, with this type of shelling, it is more difficult to pin-point the German batteries.

Yesterday a gas-driven lorry (not an ambulance) drove up to our casualty department, which is right opposite my window. It was full of casualties picked up in the street. The driver was a woman in army . . . (God, what a burst! I think I shall go to H.Q. as I'm on my own. I.D. isn't here, and Marietta is on duty.)

Sat in H.Q. for a while and came back. It's now probably about midnight. I.D. hasn't returned yet. He telephoned from town that he is waiting for the All Clear. He shouldn't do this. The first moments after the All Clear are just about the most dangerous. The Germans are waiting for nothing better than to start all over again.

What a lot of blood has been shed today! Another lorry-load

of dead bodies has arrived. From beneath the tarpaulin legs protruded, some with the bone exposed. It's a white night and one can see all this clearly.

The lorry was about to drive up to Casualty entrance, but the doctor on duty came out, glanced under the tarpaulin and gave a thumbs-down sign. The girl driver moved on to the mortuary. None of the load needed medical help any more.

I haven't finished writing about the lorry that came during the day, yesterday. In it was a boy of 14–15 years old, an apprentice maybe, badly knocked about. His face was ashen. He was bleeding copiously. Both feet had been smashed, and hung in shreds. When he was laid on the stretcher he yelled:

'Above all ... the waste of it ... I'm so young, and what have they done to me! It would be better if I'd been killed! To hell with it!'

I was struck by the word 'waste'. At first I thought I'd misheard, but no. While the boy was being carried into the building, his cries still reached me:

'It's a waste!'

The boy drank a little from the mug that Efrosiniya handed to him.

The other people on the lorry were silent. The women were taken off. One was wounded in the chest, another in the legs. Her knees were burned black from gunpowder, and monstrously bloated.

All the casualties were carried out, and only some bloodstained rags were left in the lorry.

26th July, 1943

Yesterday, again, there were many killed and wounded. The boy who had his feet torn off has died.

Important news on the radio. Mussolini has resigned.

28th July, 1943

From yesterday's stories of surgeon B.: how, during one of his operations—lancing an abscess—the blood and pus froze on his hands and covered them as tightly as a glove.

3rd August, 1943. Evening

I was nearly killed today.

At a quarter to eight, at sunset, I went to our allotment to pick some dill. I wanted to have everything ready by the time my people arrived. Marietta was at a lecture, I.D. had gone to the District Committee. I had given him my word not to go out in the street, as the shelling hadn't stopped since early morning. I promised, but our allotment isn't the street. It's right in our courtyard, on the banks of the Karpovka. I can remember when it was still a wilderness, rusty junk was buried there, remains of artificial limbs, broken-up mattresses. Now it's covered in greenery bulging like a wood seen from a plane.

It was watering time. Home Sister, girl orderlies, the up-holsterer (his cabbages are the best of all) were there. It was all so summery, peaceful. The Karpovka reflected the charm of the Botanical Gardens in its waters.

Anfisa Semenovna, the so-called 'Professor Farro', wife of the chief book-keeper, Ivan Zakharovich Krutikov, strolled between the beds. Krutikov isn't young any more. He has worked in the hospital for forty years. He has a pale narrow face and a toneless voice. He is one of the quietest people I have ever known.

Anfisa Semenovna is mentally ill. She used to work in the hospital as a pediatrician, and she suddenly went out of her mind. Since then, she is put in a mad-house during her worst periods, and at others let out, at the request of her husband. They are tenderly attached to each other, in a gentle, old-fashioned way.

Anfisa Semenovna wore a bonnet under her hat, pince-nez on her nose, and carried a small suitcase. She is energetic, talkative, domineering, knows about everything, and is, on the whole, harmless. Only she insists on being called 'Professor Farro'. She very skilfully steals keys from doors and cupboards and hides them in her little case. It's impossible to retrieve them from her, so various ruses have to be adopted.

When I came into the allotment 'Professor Farro' was just finishing something like a public lecture on how the rats, which were nibbling the turnips, allegedly spread typhoid.

I gathered some dill, and had just bent down towards a large ripe marrow when there was a noise like a thunder-clap. It was a shell falling near the second surgical. It was followed by a second—in our allotment, this time—and then a third.

I saw (so far I'd only seen such a thing so close in a movie) a pillar of fire, smoke and earth—all of it from base to crumbling apex. Hot air blew in my face. I squatted down on the bed, trying to hide my head amongst the big leaves . . . I don't remember any more—what and how. Later, when things quietened down, I picked the marrow, after all, and ran towards home, my legs shaking.

As I ran, people came running towards me from the second surgical ward, shouting that Krutikov had been injured in another distant part of the allotment. He was carrying a can to water his cucumbers. His left hand was torn off. Later, more wounded were brought to us from the street.

And what is so disturbing is the fact that the Germans seem to have found the range for our hospital. The last few days they have been getting closer and closer, more and more accurate. Now they are hitting their target.

At present the night around me is quiet, close, cloudy and brooding. There is a continual rumble of gun-fire in the distance.

We thought we might go elsewhere to spend the night, but we dropped the idea.

It doesn't matter now.

4th August, 1943

Krutikov died last night. It wasn't only that his hand had been torn off, he was also wounded in the stomach, though this wasn't noticed at once. The main hit was the watering can. Ivan Zakharovich was drenched in water.

After his hand had been dressed Krutikov said in his quiet voice that he felt pain in his stomach. He was undressed and it was found that a tiny fragment had pierced his abdomen. Three hours later he died.

The most dreadful thing was the way Anfisa searched for her husband. First she ran across to me and asked me if I'd seen him. I answered that I hadn't. In H.Q. they tried to assure her that the Director had sent him to check up on the allotment accounts. She replied (and quite reasonably) that a director who acts in such a way during shelling ought to be relieved of his post.

Finally, she realised the truth, found her husband in the second surgical and wouldn't leave his side. But he was already unconscious.

5th August, 1943

Most important announcement on the radio. We have liberated
Orel and Belgorod. In honour of this, Moscow gave a salute—a
salvo from one hundred and twenty guns. We, unfortunately,
didn't hear it. We only looked at the clock and said, 'It's
happening now.'

6th August, 1943

My lecture didn't go off too badly. There were a great many
people. Our front-line members came.

I prepared myself well. I read through once again everything
that had been written during the war by Leningrad poets, both
in the city and at the Front. (Just remembered how last spring,
at the initiative of Ketlinskaya, we went with her to the
Karelian Isthmus to pay a visit to the Army, arranged there a
'visiting meeting' and admitted to membership of the Writers'
Union Mikhail Dudin, who was working in the divisional
newspaper.)

In my report I said how every public event confronts us
writers, at first in general outline, without details, almost without contours. It's like an island seen from the ship, but the
nearer we get to it, the more clearly we can see that it is a whole
continent and begin to pick out the details. (Here I cited those
who in my opinion stayed at the initial non-contour stage in the
depicting of the war. And didn't develop further.)

I also spoke about the 'ill-willed inertia', which at times
develops within us, as quickly as weeds, and makes us repeat
ourselves, whereas our readers have outstripped us and expect
something new.

I talked about the purity of language, about composition,
about choosing a theme, about editing, the ability to change
what had to be changed. Not for nothing has it been said that
'Apollo is the God of perfection'. Rarely, much too rarely, do
we go to enough trouble in a number of things to feel the
presence of this God. (Later, after the lecture, I remembered a
splendid Indian proverb, 'Only patience can turn a mulberry
leaf into silk'.)

The lecture was long and detailed. In conclusion I said: 'We
have convinced ourselves of the power of poetry, of its efficacy.
This has been proved by the letters from our readers. Our

books are being taken amongst personal belongings to the Front; they are carried in field bags, and read before an attack.

'Therefore, let us do our utmost so that the poetry of the Fatherland War (in particular the poetry of Leningrad) should be worthy of that great goal it serves—the destruction of Fascism and the triumph of justice.'

A discussion on the lecture will take place tomorrow.

On our way back, in a *Leningrad Pravda* car, we got right in the middle of some shelling in the Liteiny Prospekt. Shells were falling from right and left. Once again, I saw pillars smoking from base to apex—not black, as in our allotment, but yellow and red, depending on whether the houses they hit were made of stone or of brick.

A terrifying roar was shaking the street, everyone was running, bent double. Many people were lying on the ground at the tram stop. (I remembered Natasha's story of how during a shelling a soldier pressed her head to the ground and covered it with his briefcase.) For a moment we hesitated; should we jump out and hide in a gateway, should we drive on as quickly as possible? Decided on the latter.

In the uproar and wreckage we passed along the Liteiny (three women huddled together in the car), came out on to the Nevsky, and from there bewildered people were running straight towards the shells.

On top of everything, the driver nearly finished us off at the cross-roads. It seemed to him that a car was coming straight at us from a side road, whereas, in actual fact, having seen us, it stopped.

I got home and soon I.D. came running from the District Committee. He was frightened. He had been told that the 'Volodarsky carré'* was under shell-fire, just the carré where, as a single dot, was I.

What sort of vengeance will Leningrad have to suffer now from the Germans, after Orel and Belgorod?

7th August, 1943

Yesterday, late in the evening, our Writers' Conference ended in 'thunder and lightning'.

Vishnevsky took me home in his car. My thoughts were full

* For defence identification purposes the city map was divided into squares.

of the conference which had just ended, and I didn't immediately notice that in our courtyard I was walking on glass splinters, a solid mass of them, as if on leaves made of glass.

When I looked carefully, I saw that the little lodge at our gates, where the time board was kept, was in ruins. This brick, one-storey building had two direct hits. No one was injured. everyone had left.

I looked at the ruins, and I remembered how I sat in the Presidium getting ready for the concluding speech, listening to the distant gun-fire. And I wondered which ill-fated district was getting it.

It turned out to be our district, even our courtyard.

8th August, 1943

I'm on my own. I.D. and Marietta have gone to town to get food. Today it is warm. Quite a summer day, Sunday.

The mad 'Professor Farro' has hidden the keys from all the safes and cupboards, where the money and ledgers of the late Krutikov were kept, and she won't give them up. Scores of cunning ruses have been used so far without success. I.D. is in a state of anguish.

9th August, 1943

Yesterday we had the worst of all Leningrad shellings. Shells fell with diabolical precision in the centre of the city, mainly at the Nevsky and Sadovaya street-crossing by the tram-stop. Crowds of people were swarming there at the time—on a Sunday. It all happened a few minutes after I.D. and Marietta, laden with food, got on to a number 3 tram and moved off. The very first shell hit a number 12 tram which was behind them. There were twenty-eight killed and sixty-two wounded.

10th August, 1943

Now summer is waning already. The first yellow leaves are covering the asphalt in our grounds. Daily, the threatening and monotonous whine of the shells (just now as well). An involuntary fear of streets. Great urge to keep near house entrances and gateways in order to take cover at the very first shell. And I'm not the only one to be like this. . . . Hard. Very hard to bear.

11th August, 1943

Outside, a fine autumn rain. Autumn. Well, God be with this summer, let it go with no regrets! As Efrosiniya Ivanovna said, 'We didn't see the pretty* summer, only saw red blood flowing.'

Today, ten to fifteen minutes after I got back, an artillery barrage began. Altogether there were six or seven shells. One burst in Leo Tolstoy Street opposite the Roentgen Institute, a second behind the allotments opposite the school, and a third in our own grounds almost on the spot where Krutikov lost his life.

People say it's the Germans aiming at the pirometer factory for precision instruments, which is working again.

News cameraman K. told me some terrifying details of the Sunday shelling of the Nevsky and Sadovaya streets: the tramway-stop was bathed in blood. Bits of bodies were lying in the street all mixed up with cans, shopping bags, spades, vegetables. Many people were on their way to the allotments outside the city, or on their way back. K. saw a torn-off arm with a cigarette in the fingers, still smoking. Beetroots and carrots were swimming in blood. Later, firemen hosed down the streets and pavements to wash the blood away.

I must frankly admit that I'm very much afraid of this tram-stop. It was a favourite target even at the time when shelling was still a rarity.

12th August, 1943

Already the search is beginning for relations or friends who failed to turn up at home or at work.

Doctor S., who is sick herself, is searching for her daughter. The Public Library is searching for one of its officials. Natasha for the engineer K., a friend of her son, who lives in her flat. He hasn't returned for three days now.

I'm writing this and thinking that at any moment the events of yesterday will repeat themselves. I must go to town. And I am afraid to go. I remember the words of the orderly, Nastya: 'It would be better for us to push against them with all our might. Either we all die or shift the Germans. This way—it's no life at all.'

* In Russian 'red' can denote pretty.

13th August, 1943

It is raining outside. The clouds are grey. I love all this. Am getting ready to go to Moscow.

18th August, 1943. Moscow

Well—here is Moscow. The flight was wonderful. We were comfortable and treated with deference. On the way to the airport the city looked strange—empty, floodlit by the moon which outshone even the brilliance of the searchlights. There were 'chandeliers' of rockets on the horizon—about seven motionless balls of light were suspended in the sky.

In Moscow the autumn is cold, but the people are warm and tender towards me.

24th August, 1943. Moscow

Yesterday evening, at nine o'clock, in honour of the liberation of Kharkov, twenty salvoes were fired from 224 guns. The whole sky sparkled with hundreds of rockets and multi-coloured tracer bullets. There were dots, dashes, lines and little balls. Gun-fire blazed round the city. Jeanne and I stood at the window of my hotel room on the ninth floor. Below us, the courtyard was bathed in blue light, spots of lights of different colours moved rapidly along the walls, reflected in the glass of the windows on the many storeys. Applause from the street floated up to us on the ninth floor.

5th September, 1943

No, after all, it's a very good thing that I did come here. It has brought to an end the mental state I have been in lately, when my mind was numb and apprehensive.

8th September, 1943

Important news. Italy has capitulated. So far there has been no official announcement, but it is true. We have taken Stalino in the Donetz Basin.

9th September, 1943

This morning, at six o'clock, the capitulation of Italy was announced on the radio.

23rd September, 1943

The day of departure is approaching. I am completing my affairs. Only, I haven't managed to write anything: I lost myself in a whirl of activities.

8.40 in the evening

We have liberated Poltava. We shall watch the salute in the rain today. So far, this hasn't happened. . . .

There was a salute—and without rain. There was low cloud and because of this the noise was greater. It was majestic and sombre.

The second salute for the town of Unecha was in the rain this time. Scarlet and green reflections gleamed in the wet, mirror-like asphalt.

24th September, 1943. Moscow

A splendid business day. Succeeded in everything I did, and managed to do everything. It seems I'll fly back on Tuesday.

Today, when I was in the Soviet Information Bureau, I was utterly shaken. It seemed that the map of the whole world has opened up for me, from Sweden to Egypt. Everywhere I am being read.

I must write more, mainly prose. I want to be read everywhere, and to be loved by the friends of my country.

25th September, 1943. Moscow

The Germans are running faster than the French did in 1812. Today we have liberated Smolensk and Yaroslavl. The salute was twentyfold from 224 guns.

Smolensk is free! . . . This means that the Germans are no longer in a position to hold the defence of the Dnieper.

And what will happen at Kiev? What will happen to Leningrad, that is the main thing? Does it mean that it too will be free some day?

How I long to be there! To feel glad—that is to be there already!

26th September, 1943. Moscow

I have come back from Peredelkino, where I spent the whole day. Emotionally, it was easier than I expected. Maybe because it was such a lovely day—autumnal, golden. I found two mushrooms and one fungus.

The woman caretaker told me, 'Don't search, you won't find any. The war will soon be over, and that is why there are no mushrooms.'

How strange it is, this popular superstition. In the autumn, on the eve of the war, there was an unnaturally large amount of mushrooms. We gathered basketfuls on our land, and didn't know what to do with them all. The woman caretaker said: 'That means war.'

The house in Peredelkino is empty. The most important thing, there wasn't a single file of papers, not a photograph, not a diary, no newspaper cuttings—God knows what else . . . nothing was there, most likely went for lighting the stoves. It would be a good thing if it were only that. It is sad to think of my personal papers being scattered and wandering homeless, passing through strange hands, being read coldly and without understanding. I stood for a brief moment in little Mishenka's room. The nails which used to hold up a shelf were still there. I knocked his little head on it when I was taking him out of his cot.

We had dinner at Afinogenov's. His absence is much felt, and has been taken very hard. I can just see his smile, his pale blue shirt. I can hear his voice.

28th September, 1943. Moscow

Everything is ready and packed. It would be lovely to fly off tomorrow. There was no plane today. I long so much to be back in Leningrad. Vitebsk direction—that affects our city directly. One must keep on and live long enough to be alive on the day of its liberation. To the day when the Germans will either flee or be routed.

29th September, 1943. Moscow

The weather promises to be fine. If only we could get off today.

Today, the amount of energy I spend on telephone conversations would be enough to drive a small engine.

3rd October, 1943. Leningrad

We had a good flight.

The whole day we flew over autumn woods, with the blue sky growing cold overhead. It was nearly dark when we landed

in Leningrad (already the days are short), and it was in impene-
trable darkness that we drove in the coach.

During the last two days since we came back there hasn't
been any close gun-fire.

There is firing somewhere far off—and not very often at
that.

From children's conversations in 1942.

A boy asks:

'Mother, what is ham?'

The mother tells him. The boy:

'And who has tried it?'

A girl:

'Mother, what does a giant weigh? And what rations is he
getting?'

A third child had recited the poem of Lermontov, 'I swear by
the first day of Jam' (instead of 'Creation').*

The children at that time were thinking a great deal about
food . . . and the grown-ups, too, by the way.

7th October, 1943

A girl who is evacuated writes to her mother: 'I am mastering
the rifle and reading Gogol's *Dead Souls*. She enclosed a butterfly in her letter and writes: 'This butterfly is found on the
Steppes. There is no such butterfly in Leningrad,' and adds a
P.S.: 'I beg the military censorship not to throw out this
butterfly inadvertently, or to squash it.'

All this was in a letter written by the daughter of Mariya
Nikolayevna F. Mariya Nikolayevna herself managed the 'Ars'
Cinema in Leo Tolstoy Square in 1941. In November the
Germans dropped three delayed-action bombs on the building
in which the cinema was housed. True, they weren't large
bombs. After about three hours they exploded, one by one.
By this time, on orders of the anti-aircraft defence, the building
was evacuated, and there was no one in the cinema either.
Only Mariya Nikolayevna remained. She explained to me
why: the safe, with the day's takings, was her responsibility.

While Mariya Nikolayevna stayed and guarded the safe, a
colleague came and said:

'I shall remain with you.'

Mariya Nikolayevna replied:

* In Russian jam is *varenye* and creation *tvorenye*, very similar in sound.

'No, I don't want you to. You have two children and an old mother.'

Her colleague, objected:

'You have a daughter and a husband at the Front.'

So she remained. A little later the technical manager, an elderly man, joined them.

He said:

'I too shall remain with you. After all, I am a man.'

All three sat and waited for the explosion. They were shaken, covered with plaster, cut by glass, but they survived. The safe where the money was kept had been blasted into a heap of twisted metal, and it was necessary to use an electric drill to open it.

9th October, 1943

I.D. told me that when I was away, during particularly bad shellings, he carried our Kuzya in his briefcase when he went to H.Q. Now he has grown too big to get into the case.

From a medical report of Zinaida Vasilyevna:

'The child, wounded by a shell fragment, was lying on a pillow, and because of this all the wounds are filled with feathers.'

'A woman in the last month of her pregnancy was wounded. The unborn baby was wounded also.'

About a child who begs that he shall be given a 'little gas-mask' for his birthday.

In the wasteland opposite us, the children play at war. One of them commands a platoon. With a cry, 'All forces against Leshka!'—they rush at this boy, whom I don't envy.

12th October, 1943

A sentence I overheard by chance: 'At such a time, all humour must be kept on a tight rein.' Must it?

14th October, 1943

The day before yesterday a shell hit one of our buildings, a room next to Lenin's Hall (he spoke there in April 1917 on the 'April Theses').

The shelling began one minute after the students had left the premises. We got there before the brick dust had quite settled, and this altered the atmosphere of the room in a peculiar way.

It's probably what happens after a volcano has erupted. There was a gaping hole in the wall. The only thing that remained intact was a bust of Lenin on a tall plaster pedestal. Because of the dust, the colour was changed from white to a sombre grey. As if the expression of the face had changed.

Yesterday, during the Party conference in the same Lenin's Hall, the shelling started again. I.D. stopped the meeting and we all dispersed.

Today the situation at the Front is excellent. We can expect a salute today, maybe even two.

17th October, 1943

Yesterday, during a heavy shelling, I paid a visit to Casualty. They were already bringing in the wounded. A woman worker from the State Institute of Practical Surgery was one of the first to be brought in. Her right arm and right foot were wounded. She was pale and trembling with nerves, and she pressed an expensive shoe to her bosom, from her wounded foot. It was covered in blood. There was also a splinter, clearly visible, near her mouth, directly under the skin. As the doctor on duty said, 'It stuck out.' The casualty was taken straight to the X-ray department.

Later I went with Bulatov and Alventina Vasilyevna to the look-out tower on the roof of one of our buildings. It was terrifying to walk along the sloping roof wet with rain, and to climb over some taut wires. On the autumn horizon heavy flashes—beneath these, a sombre concentration of buildings. The dome of St. Isaac's, the Admiralty spire, the Peter and Paul Fortress—there are grey covers on all of them now, hiding the golden sparkle.

Bulatov said:

'If a shell should fall, lie down at once.'

This didn't become necessary. Otherwise I'm sure I could never have held on to the wet sloping roof.

On the way back we went in through another nearer window. And it seemed so cosy in the attic!

8th November, 1943

I haven't written anything for a long time. But a lot of things have happened. We have liberated Kiev. At times the approaching end of the war seems so clear that one's heart beats much faster.

I spent the festive days* very actively. Yesterday we went to the Karelian Isthmus as guests of the Army Commander, A. I. Cherepanov.

The invitation, through Vasilyevna, was of long standing. Yesterday he sent a car to fetch us. We rushed along the Kirovsky in the direction of the islands, past the Chernaya Rechka—the site of Pushkin's duel—and then Pargolovo, Toksovo, pine-clad Karelian copses and hills. Everything on its guard, silent, covered in an autumnal haze.

The Army is not engaged in active operations. Its role is that of a covering force against the Finns. But the fact that it is not engaged in waging war (it is called a 'non-fighting' army) gnaws at the heart of every soldier here, from the Army Commander to the rank-and-file private.

With their very first words everyone explains why they aren't fighting. But most likely their hour will come and they too will go into battle. In the meantime everything here is in perfect order, guns and howitzers are placed with a grim smartness. Special hideouts are constructed for them, from which they can roll out in a matter of seconds. It was proudly explained to us that local 'production experience' has already found its application with other armies.

After a rest at H.Q. the Commander drove us closer to the advanced lines three kilometres away from the Finns, from where we proceeded on foot. Although I assured him that in the winter of 1942, when I visited Fedyuninsky's army, I was four times as close to the Germans, he wasn't willing to take us any further. He explained that he was responsible for me, 'before literature'.

Later, at supper, this professional soldier put me, a professional writer, to shame by quoting verses of poets of Pushkin's galaxy that were unknown to me.

At one place the Commander pointed towards the wooded hills, blue in the mist of an early twilight, and said:

'The enemy is there.'

This peaceful autumn landscape is steeped in war. A mossy mound, a half-destroyed tent, a heap of brushwood in a clearing—all these at any moment can open fire. Quiet, silence,

* Anniversary of the October revolution.

total absence of people. And if you look closely there are permanent firing points everywhere, cunningly surrounded by wire with metal strips on it in many places. Just touch it, and the clinking and ringing starts. Anti-tank ditches stretch endlessly.

For the first time I saw a firing point; everything there is metal and concrete, nothing made of wood. It is a circular fortress with firing ports in all directions. Seats for machine-gunners are made like those on agricultural machines.

The living quarters are deep underground, and reached by descending a ladder. Commanders of firing posts and batteries reported to the Commander that they were ready to carry out their tasks, as well as reporting on the present occupations of the troops. One officer reported lucidly:

'The soldiers are busy resting'.

Two salvoes were fired in our honour by one of the batteries of heavy howitzers. The Finns replied a few minutes later. At a remote cross-roads in the woods a sentry unit came out of a small, well-hidden tent. There were two soldiers: one a Belorussian, or maybe Ukranian, bearded, not young, intense. The other was dark with an aquiline nose and had the light movements of a highlander.

The Commander treated them both to cigarettes, and turning their backs on the Finnish side, they smoked in secret.

We returned to Leningrad late at night, lit by a waning moon.

Now I can visualise the Blockade ring from almost every side.

26th November, 1943

Once more I rewrote almost all of the concluding part of the poem. And in point of fact finished it. Tomorrow I am going to see Ostroumova-Lebedeva to decide on the design of the book. After that I could embark on some prose.

Prose, of course, will present its own difficulties, but there won't be that frenzy that hits us when one is writing poetry.

I shall make sure that the energy that kept me working so hard this year carries on into 1944 without interruption, so that there isn't that dreadful feeling of 'starting in a vacuum'.

Smoothly—smoothly, and it will move and move. . . .

12th December, 1943

At last the Ozerskys have arrived from Krasnoyarsk. Part of the Institute was evacuated there in the spring of 1942, after it had been to Kislovodsk.

Now that the main wartime difficulties are behind us, I.D. has thought it possible to ask if he may be freed from his duties as Director, and put forward Professor Ozersky as his successor. It coincides with the wish of Nikolai Ivanovich himself. Thus everything is settled satisfactorily.

Now I.D. will be able to return to his beloved history of medicine. Large tomes from the library, small books and sets of old medical journals have already made their appearance in our room. Already Kuzya, our cat, sleeps on the card-index boxes.

I.D. is happy and so am I. I shan't have to hear about 'fan' tubes and 'stop'-cocks. A full stop has been put to this.

17th December, 1943

Yesterday evening we went for our usual walk. The night was warm, damp and slippery, in spite of the fact that both Ozerskys maintained they saw the Aurora Borealis.

In Leo Tolstoy Square we wanted to have a closer look at the bakery which had been hit by a shell during the day, but the light of our small torch was naturally not strong enough for us to see anything.

We just managed to get home when three or four shells crashed one after the other into the Square.

Yesterday afternoon our former student, now post-graduate, Orshanskaya was fatally wounded there. Her intestines have been torn, her pulse is non-existent, there is no hope at all.

In the same shelling a very young second-year student, Verochka Berezovskaya, was killed outright. I.D. saw her ten minutes before her death; she was leaving the anatomy theatre where examinations were taking place. I.D. asked her:

'Well, are you shaking with nerves?'

She answered:

'Others are shaking today. It's my turn tomorrow.'

And an hour later she was lying in the mortuary.

19th December, 1943

This morning we went to the funeral of Verochka Berezovskaya. The morning was clear, rose-coloured and dry. As we approached the mortuary, a lorry carrying the coffins of some seamen, also killed by a shell, moved off. A squad of Baltic sailors marched behind the lorry.

We got into the small 'leave-taking' room with difficulty.* There was one other coffin—a woman's, covered with muslin. She had also been killed by a shell. And there too was Berezovskaya's little coffin. Only a waxen, adolescent hand was showing through a heap of artificial roses and lilies. As they took leave of the dead girl, everyone kissed the little hand.

The head of the coffin was draped in tulle. When I wanted to throw this back and see her face, people whispered to me that the back of her skull was all that remained of her head. The mother bore herself with fortitude, but her father . . . one could truly say that he was killed by grief.

I.D. with some girl students carried out the coffin. The lorry went first to Skorokhodov Street and there it stopped in front of the tidy little house that is the Stomatological Clinic. Berezovsky father is in charge there, and Verochka worked here as a sister, when she was a medical student. Benches were taken from the clinic and put into the lorry for the journey to the cemetery and here, in the street, a small meeting was held.

I.D. was the first speaker. He was followed by workers and colleagues from the clinic, and finally by a girl student. Guns rumbled incessantly—and somewhere, in a street nearby, a funeral march was being played. They were burying a soldier.

The sky was clear, beautiful—a young, tender winter's day —a long-awaited slight frost, essential for the start of our offensive.

When she heard the guns Berezovskaya's mother said: 'So long as we get to the cemetery.'

And it wasn't clear whether she was afraid for herself or whether she was anxious to bury her daughter in peace and quiet.

* In Russia a funeral is a ceremony consisting of two parts: the carrying out of the body, to which all mourners assemble and which is mentioned here, and the funeral cortège taking the coffin for burial at the cemetery.

Evening

An important announcement on the radio. An enormous break-through of the German defence line in the Nevel area. It's clear now why the Germans have been in such a fury these last few days.

25th December, 1943

There was a meeting of the Party Bureau, also a general meeting. I was accepted by the Party. On Monday the Bureau of the District Committee meets. Early this morning Marietta and I dropped in to the District Committee to clarify our statements. My year is ending well.

28th December, 1943

An anxious day . . . I was about to leave for the District Committee to clarify the questionnaire—a barrage of shelling in our district. I.D. has gone to town on business and won't be back till evening, and this worries me very much. We had a tiff before he left and didn't say good-bye to each other. And one ought not to part without saying good-bye in Leningrad.

As soon as the shelling quietens down, we shall go to the District Committee.

29th December, 1943

A restless, grim night. Shelling from heavy guns was resumed three times. Shells fell very near at the House of Industrial Co-operation. Our building swayed like a house of cards, but we didn't go down or even put on our clothes. I only took my pillow and moved to the sofa, away from the windows.

British raids on Berlin are consoling.

Evening

The Bureau of the District Committee held its meeting at an oval table in a large beautiful room. The floor was covered with runners and the table with green baize. I was asked questions, and I stood up to answer.

Question: Why didn't you join the Party Organisation of the Writers' Union?

Answer: The Leningrad branch of the Writers' Union has at present no Party Organisation of its own. Front-line writers are attached to the Military Party organisations—others to factories, where they work.

Question: What kind and what amount of public work have you done during this time?

Answer: I have spoken and read in factories, clubs, army units, hospitals and schools.

Question: How do you visualise your Party work in the future?

Answer: As before, I shall write and speak. But I shall endeavour to do it much better, from the point of view of the highest literary standard. Besides that, I shall do everything that the Party may demand of me.

Question: Are you not frightened by the strict Party discipline?

Answer: No, it doesn't frighten me. I am by nature an organised person.

On the way home from the District Committee, I asked myself, How, then, really has the year of my probation* passed? What changes have I undergone during this span of time?

I have read and spoken in factories and works, in army and naval units. I have written. True enough. But I was doing all this before. Where, then, lies the difference?

It's not that easy to formulate, but there is a difference. Previously it was like this: Suppose I wrote something successful—I was glad. Failure was bitter to me, but the joy or the sadness were for myself alone.

Now, however, I think: To what extent does my writing enhance the cause of Soviet literature, which in its turn is only part of a great cause—the flowering of my country, the first Socialist country in the world?

Every literary work, extended logically, must transform itself into action, or, at any rate, be capable of such transformation. I tried to think this out, to guess what is happening behind the springboard at the end of the page, from where life takes off.

What impact do my verses have at present? How did my pen, my weapon, work in besieged Leningrad? Was my work needed at least to some degree by it? I'm responsible for it.

That was the task entrusted to me by the Party. It is my Party business.

* As a candidate for membership of the Communist Party.

M *

30th December, 1943

A quiet night. It was only late in the evening that a continuous rumble was audible. Maybe they are our 'Katyushas'* talking. Radio reports are excellent.

. . . Today we have the first blizzard of the year.

31st December, 1943

Thus the year is ending. The one about to arrive holds out the promise of victory for us. Yesterday's announcements were stupendous. We listened too, in rapture, to news of the 'most ferocious' raid on Berlin. There is no hell bad enough for the Germans.

1st January, 1944

We saw the New Year in at Ketlinskaya's. The journey home was lovely, we walked across the whole of the quiet city, which is lightly covered in snow, and valses on the radio floated out of the windows. Walking in the streets was allowed up to two in the morning and by that time we were home.

I wish good health to myself! If there is health, then there is a book.

2nd January, 1944

Story about a Militiaman (one of Efrosiniya Ivanovna's tales):

A woman in a queue scolded her child so roughly, pulling it by its arm so hard, that people were enraged and called in a Militiaman.

He arrived, found out what was the matter, took the child by the hand and started to lead it away. The mother was taken aback.

'Where are you taking him?'

'To my wife. She understands how to treat children.'

'And is it your business to interfere with my child?'

'What else? The State has put me here to keep order. Well—that's what I'm doing.'

Yesterday the Students' 'New Year's Fir Tree'† party took place in Lenin's Hall. The hall was filled to bursting with

---

* This name, endearment for Catherine, was given to a multi-rocket firing device introduced by the Soviet Army.

† Replaced the former traditional Christmas tree.

students, men and girls, also sailors, under the patronage of
the Institute.* They were smartened up, polished to the hilt,
obviously eager to dance until an alert called them to their
ships, no matter how long this peaceful pause might last.

Against their naval jackets, the girls' dresses seemed so thin,
so bright. Wherever did these dresses come from? By what
miracle had they been preserved? Had they been hidden in
secret places, safe from bombs or shells, rolled up into cocoons?
Had they lain there for over two years in order to flutter out on
this New Year's Eve, lit by the fir tree's electric garlands? (Real
candles were strictly forbidden by the city's Fire Defence.)

A few fancy-dress costumes circled the tree. One girl even
had a fan, though God knows the temperature of the hall gave
her no justification for this.

A boy, Yura, wore a pierrot costume, stretched by his loving
mother over cotton-wool underclothing. The first winter of
the Blockade, Yura was too weak and undernourished to leave
his room. The second winter we could see him on skis in our
courtyard, and now he is darting among the dancers like a
little imp, the personification of gaiety and naughtiness.

It was Yura who informed us that in addition to the radiogram (What's a radiogram? So what!) there will be a real live
jazz band as well.

And, in fact, a Valtorna, a violin and a saxophone turned up.

The lights in the ceiling were turned off, only the fir tree
blazed, and it was enormous. The students themselves had
brought it in a lorry from the woods. It was gaily decorated
with a star on top, covered with gold and silver tinsel.

The jazz band struck up. Confetti was strewn, the couples
began to dance.

There wasn't any shelling.

4th January, 1944

A lecture on the radio about 'flu was interrupted by the
announcement of shelling. In the morning there had been a
few heavy explosions, but I heard them only vaguely. They were
all somehow mixed up with my dreams.

* This patronage, called in the Soviet Union in Russian *shefstvo*—sponsor-
ship, forms a link and entails voluntary assistance of the organisation
or body which assumes the patronage towards the one which is under it.

What exhaustion because of all this! What a high ceiling of tension! When will there be an end to the Leningrad days of hardship?

6th January, 1944

The Radio Committee still wants 'first and second trumpeters and a piccolo flautist'. This is being announced morning and evening—but there aren't any: they died out in the time of our hunger.

Words of I.D.:

'I walk to my Herzen Institute as if I were on the rim of a trench, the street is so well marked.'

A professor, about the students:

'They ought to carry logs for warmth, and they occupy themselves with qualitative analysis.'

9th January, 1944

Yesterday we liberated Kirovograd (formerly Elizavetgrad). The very place where a long time ago my father made me flee and save myself with my mother and little Jeanne from the same Germans. Then their ships *Goeben* and *Breslau* were shelling Odessa.

In Leningrad blood is still shed; it's a seven-day-a-week war. Shellings, victims, direct hits on trams, as it happened on Wednesday to a number 10. Inside it, seventy people alone were killed.

All is quiet on our front. But hell can break loose at any time, though the Germans cling ferociously to Polotsk and Vitebsk, key points of Leningrad's fate.

I am about to start writing a leaflet for the Front for the anniversary of last year's break-through of the Blockade.

12th January, 1944

Alena Oserskaya has brought a spinning wheel back from her evacuation at Krasnoyarsk. The women there taught her to spin, and in the evening she spins, only breaking off in order to play a Beethoven sonata, or work over her thesis for a dissertation on 'antiquities'.

14th January, 1944

No matter how hard it is at times to endure the monotonous, nerve-racking way of life in Leningrad, it will be necessary to stay here till the spring. During this time the fate of the city must be settled—and for better. Frosts have set in. Events are in the air. New wounded have appeared here: an important indication.

15th January, 1944.

A continuous rumble, of greater strength than we have heard before, shakes the air from early morning. These are our naval guns, people say, from the district of Oranienbaum.

The rumble goes on. Bulatov told me that this is 'us softening his advanced lines'.

What is going to happen? Can it be that we shan't succeed this time either? But everyone believes that all will be well. People wear very special faces.

In the morning, at a critical time as usual, Professor Garshin appeared—'just to drop in' because his feelings were too much for him.

I must get down to writing!

Dear God, what a din! Some gun-fire! . . . I.D. is saying already that I must go to Pushkin as soon as it is freed. (Oh God, what a noise!)

19th January, 1944

It has already been officially announced that 'On the Leningrad front our troops have switched to the offensive to the south of Oranienbaum. The offensive continues.'

The same has happened on the Volkhov front as well. That means it has really 'started'! But how many wounded are there in all the Leningrad hospitals! And those huge black red-cross buses move in an endless procession to the stations, to collect the wounded . . . So long as their blood is not flowing in vain!

20th January, 1944

Yesterday we liberated Krasnoye Selo, Ropsha, Peterhof and Duderhof.

At last the 'Leningrad Salute' has roared in Moscow.

21st January, 1944

Uritsk, Ligovo, Strelna and Novgorod have been freed by us. In other places, 'German troops have been surrounded and are being exterminated'. Now is Pushkin's turn.

22nd January, 1944

Yesterday morning, Sunday, I was telephoned to first by the Writers' Union and then by the Political Administration of the Leningrad front, to be ready: in an hour, we are going on a tour of the liberated places.

It started at once, behind the Kirov works. There, everything is ploughed over by war. Barbed wire, bunches of electrical wiring, ditches, the brown debris of destroyed houses everywhere. Long tongues of soot radiate out on the snow from bomb craters, the strength of the flames can be determined by them—that is the 'softening up of the enemy's forward lines' by our air force.

Of the old clinic of Forel only the walls remain. The tragic ruins of Pishmash (a typewriter factory) against the winter sky. The Germans converted it into a powerful fort, and from it they shelled the city.

There were still shields with German inscriptions on road crossings everywhere, arrows, drawings of elephants— symbols of happiness, or what? Little bridges, even the most insignificant, were blown up. Both our drivers took great care in crossing the newly constructed temporary bridges. At the approach to each bridge round mines lie on planks in rows. They have already been defused. Other mines, longer, with feathery tails, are piled in heaps and look like dead fish.

To left and right of the road, sappers march in the snow in chain formation, each leading a dog on a leash. We were told about one of these dogs who discovered forty-five mines during yesterday alone. But the highway isn't safe yet. A 'pick-up' preceding us struck a mine, luckily only touching it with the rim of a wheel. But still the driver was slightly wounded, and blood flowed down his face. He shouted to us:

'And where the hell do you think you're going? Can't you see for yourselves what is happening?'

But we were driven safely through.

In Strelna a field kitchen was already smoking under the

palace arch, and our soldiers were carrying water in pails captured from the Germans and they were chopping wood with their axes. The echo rang out as if it were glad that once again it was repeating peaceful sounds.

The park at Strelna is practically devastated. Hardly any of the trees are undamaged. One tree—battered, frightening, its bare branches upright—seemed to grip its head in the wounded branches in an attitude that was almost human.

We had to move with caution, and not to leave the well-trodden paths because mines were everywhere.

I took away from Strelna a large piece of German green anti-mustard gas paper.

Peterhof Palace is damaged so badly that it will be beyond human effort to restore it. Climbing over the wreckage we came on what remained of the great terrace, and looked for a long while on the dead 'Avenue of Fountains' descending towards the sea.

In the clear winter air a German gun could be seen in the lower part of the park. It was on a semicircular platform, right at the parapet. It faced Kronstadt on the other side of the Gulf. It is not possible yet to go near this gun, because all the ground in between is mined. I remembered when we stood at the mooring at Kronslot, looking at distant Peterhof, and the Commander said: 'The time will come . . .'

We didn't reach Krasnoye Selo until it was almost evening. In the outskirts where a sign hung which said 'Kingisep', by the light of a burning house we saw German prisoners of war. They wore camouflaged garments and were dirty and unshaven. They were being led along a way shown by an arrow and a sign saying 'To Leningrad'.

They were the first Germans I had seen during the whole of the war.

24th January, 1944

We have liberated Pushkin and Pavlovsk.

27th January, 1944

The greatest event in the life of Leningrad—complete liberation from the Blockade. And here words fail me, a professional writer. I simply say Leningrad is free. And there isn't any more to be said.

28th January, 1944

Yesterday evening, at eight o'clock, by the order of General Govorov, we had a grand salute, of a kind only given on days of the greatest victories. We had twenty-four salvoes from 324 guns. The city of Lenin saluted the troops of the Leningrad front. But our rockets were fired in a newer and prettier way than in Moscow. All different colours were fired at once, there. And here it was done in such a way that now only green rockets were hurled upwards, and then the whole sky was lit by a phosphorescent light, as if a meteor had flown past; now there was a plethora of crimson lights, now golden stars streamed downwards, like ears of grain from an invisible bracket . . . all this fell and burnt out on the ice of the Neva.

They were military rockets and we had seen them before. Their role was to signal the beginning of an attack, mark out landing places for aircraft, signal gunners, direct infantry, warn tanks. But then they were fired as single rockets, and now— thousands of attacks, hundreds of air battles, sorties, naval engagements rushed into the sky all at once. Most striking were the ships' searchlights (which they didn't have in Moscow). In particular, one from below, directed at the spire of the Peter and Paul tower, straight at the angel, was so strong it seemed solid. It looked like a sloping white tower or a bridge up which one could walk to the angel itself.

Another searchlight lit up the building of the Stock Exchange, from afar, in a dramatic way. Now it was seen in its entirety on the end of a beam, now splitting the columns or the façade, now plunging it all into darkness. The entire sky was criss-crossed by searchlights.

Guns were raised on naval vessels and along the embankment, left and right. Just before the sound of the salvo, little tongues of flame shot out of the barrels, the way hell-fire is shown on old pictures.

During the radio announcement about the salute, I was speaking at a meeting of Intelligentsia at our District Committee. I finished just ten minutes before the salute started.

I dressed quickly and jumped on to a number 3 tram. It was very crowded, everyone was hurrying to the Kirov Bridge. We arrived just in time for the first salvo.

The Kirov Bridge and the Marsovo Pole* were completely filled with people. A newsreel van stood by the Suvorov monument and filming was in progress. Motor-cycles, cycles, pedestrians were all mixed up. Armoured cars and sometimes a tank were moving slowly here and there, amongst the traffic.

The salvoes were quite terrific, a true 'Thunder of Victory'. The great dazzling light amazed us. All our faces were lifted towards the sky, and the features lit to the smallest detail.

30th January, 1944

Two hours after the salute, in our maternity department, K. gave birth to a boy. A child of Leningrad who was born free.

1st February, 1944

Went yesterday to Duderhof, Gatchina, Pavlovsk and Pushkin, in a party consisting of painters and museum officials. We went past Pulkovo on the way back.

Last time I saw Pulkovo Observatory was through the end of a toy stereoscope. There, with touching accuracy, white buildings showed against the greenery, including the main observatory block built by Bryulov, the tall main tower where the big telescope was housed, and the library where the history of all the stars was kept.

Now all this has been burned, shot to smithereens, bombed, destroyed. Only a few charred trees remained in what used to be the park. The buildings are in ruins. The entire Pulkovo Hill is churned up with dugouts and trenches. They are ours, but the Germans were close by on the other side of the hill. Their dugouts and trenches were literally face to face with our units, but, in spite of that, the Germans failed.

The ruined Pulkovo passed before us at the end of a short winter's day, like a sombre vision.

Duderhof (Crow's Mountain)—its shape is reminiscent of a flat-iron. It was from Duderhof that the Germans corrected their artillery shelling of the city. One can imagine how hard it must have been for our units to capture those icy slopes. Tanks wouldn't be much use here. The infantry must have stormed the hill and taken it.

Women employees of the three former museums—the

* Champs de Mars.

Pavlovsk, the Gatchina and the Pushkin—were in our coach, and it was quite something to see the reunion of these officials with their museums, and to hear their exclamations. 'The Dutch village is intact!' 'The little bridge is safe!' 'The Venus Pavilion is still there!' But more often they remained silent, because nothing recognisable was left.

I didn't get into the Pavlovsk Palace—only looked at it from afar. The bridge over the river Slavyanka, like all the other bridges, was blown up by the Germans. We had to scramble down a steep cliff and walk across frozen logs. This was difficult for me.

But a girl from the Pavlovsk Museum ran down and up the steep icy slope on the other side with such speed that the men could hardly catch up with her. She came back slowly, and her face was so pale that it was noticeable, even in the freezing air. She told us that the Palace was nothing but a shell now, only its silhouette remained. It's all ruined inside.

At Gatchina there used to be a granite ball on the top of a tall obelisk at the entrance to the park. The Germans knocked it off and mounted an enormous swastika. But when we came to the park the swastika, derivisely fouled by crows, had already been knocked down by our soldiers, and was lying at the base of the obelisk.

In the opinion of the museum staff, at least some architectural features—general layout—remained of the Palace of Gatchina. The general appearance of the building, its original design, the proportions of its component parts. The Germans hadn't intended to surrender Gatchina. On the contrary, people were driven to it from Strelna and Peterhof. At the last moment, when our troops were already entering the town, the Germans poured an inflammable fluid over the Palace and set it on fire. A sheet of flame burst out of every window, leaving a trail of black soot on the outside walls. The whole building now stood decked out in funeral plumes. When we were there, some of the beams were still smouldering.

Inside, chaos reigned. Ruins, collapsed ceilings. In Czar Paul's room a fireplace was dangling in the air. Over the fireplace an antique carving, dating from the first century B.C., depicting the sacrifice of the Emperor Titus. In another room, also overhead over a doorway, a bas relief of a marble lobster. You have to look up at these things, throwing your head backwards, but you must be careful not to fall through a hole in the floor at the same time.

At the front of the Palace, next to the main entrance, two allegorical statues of Italian origin, War and Peace. Both remained intact in their wooden casings. The Gatchina Museum worker was as delighted with these statues as if they had been living people. She had hidden them in their coverings herself.

On the pediment of the Palace building it says: 'Founded on the 30th May, 1766. Completed in the year 1781.' Now one could add: 'Destroyed by the Germans in January in the year 1944.'

On one of the Gatchina walls a German inscription in indelible pencil: 'We were here.' And further on: 'When Ivan comes, everything here will be empty', and the address: 'Richard Wurf, Stettin, Uhland Strasse 2, and the telephone, D.28–10–43.'

I wonder where this man Wurf is now? (His name means 'a toss'.) Was it he perhaps who was 'tossed' out into the snow-covered road between Gatchina and Pavlovsk, barefoot, half his head smashed in, a lump of blood-stained ice where his eyes had been, his head forced back. From beneath the snow we could see a chevron on the sleeve: 'S.S.' We had seen many such corpses.

Inside Gatchina itself—disgusting, dreadful traces of the German way of life. A prison surrounded twice by barbed wire, an officers' club, shop signs in German and Russian: 'Commission Shop', 'Bakery', and the owners' names: Eisen, Maslyanikov.

When Gatchina was liberated, our troops found about four thousand people there. We met a man in rags, thin, pale, with a bandaged arm; he couldn't look enough at us who came from Leningrad.

On the deserted road, and at the bridges, life had already started again. True, so far it is a nomadic, military one. Small camp fires are burning, snow water is being heated in mess tins. In one place it was evident a horse had just been slaughtered, and the offal, bright blue, crimson and scarlet (all the guts are enormous), lay in a heap in the snow.

At another crossing there was a field office under the sky, a writing desk and a chair stood, carried out from a former German dugout. A man wearing a tall fur hat had some ink in a little tin. He was blowing on it anxiously, warming it with his breath.

Two of our small tanks lay half frozen in the Izhora river. Written on them: 'For Leningrad' and 'Suvorov'. Both tanks had been knocked over, and ice-cold water was constantly washing their wounds, covering them with rust the colour of blood.

As we were entering Pushkin Park, Evgeniya Leonidovna, the former local guide, shouted in rapture:

'The ruins are intact!'

And true enough the artificial romantic ruins of Catherine the Great's time remained in a perfect state of preservation.

In the Palace itself, despite the warnings of a sapper with his dog, Evgeniya Leonidovna rushed through all the rooms, large and small halls, galleries and passages. She looked into places that were inaccessible from the courtyard. We tried to follow her as far as we could.

I was the first to enter the basement of the Cameron Gallery. I walked in with a quick, confident stride, but I jumped out pretty fast on tiptoe. Three aerial bombs as large as barrels were lying on the floor. They had already been defused, but I didn't know that. Altogether there were eleven such bombs, each weighing a ton. They were laid out in the Palace and in the park, connected with wires. They were supposed to blow up at the last moment, but the Germans had no time to set them off.

In the side basement there was a heap of torn shoes—a cobblers' workshop. The German soldiers' living quarters were downstairs too. From upstairs they had dragged down sofas upholstered in damask, satin-covered armchairs, vases, carpets. Everything was covered in a thick layer of dirt and soot.

Also they had no time to carry away the precious parquet flooring from the Great Hall. They merely prised it up in great chunks, ready for despatch. The whole of the Hall of Mirrors is smashed to bits, half burned, ruthlessly damaged. The roof is open to the sky. The decorated ceilings hang down in tatters, and instead of a bright blue painted sky, the cold winter sky looks down on us, dimly. The entire hall is littered with fragments of the mirrors, and of gesso carvings, made by patient serfs.

The Alexandrovsky Palace, though completely empty, was

nevertheless in a better state. A Spanish unit had been quartered here, that was plain from the Carmencitas drawn in charcoal on the walls. They had hats trimmed with roses, fans and high combs in their hair.

In the Round Hall the Spaniards had a kind of chapel. They constructed a bizarre 'altar', which still remained there. It was made from odd pieces of furniture, amongst which Evgeniya Leopoldovna immediately recognised a Chinese bookshelf from the room of the late Empress Mariya Fedorovna.

It was time to return to Leningrad. Once more, we walked past the palaces and the Pushkin High School.* Some of the avenues in the park are practically undamaged. Shadows of the trees turned blue on the snow.

On the way back, when we were practically in town, we saw a large party of about three hundred German prisoners.

2nd February, 1944

Unexpected news: Tomorrow I am going to Moscow to attend our plenary session.

5th February, 1944. Moscow

The plenary meeting started yesterday. We travelled to Moscow without changing trains—straight from the Oktiybrskaya Station. It isn't the 'Arrow'† yet, but already it's a through train.

17th February, 1944. Moscow

My time in Moscow flies as usual, at a frantic speed. Many encounters, friendly talks, readings and speeches. My future is rosy, but the present is overshadowed by illness. Physically, I feel rotten. You need an iron constitution in order to be happy.

20th February, 1944. Moscow

A plan has sprung up. It is for me to go back to Leningrad, there to wait for the first 'Arrow' train—which is just about to be re-started. I'm to come back on it to Moscow and write about it in *Pravda*. I shall most likely do just that—keep my hotel room, go and come back.

* A special high school for the children of courtiers and the nobility.
† 'Red Arrow', a night train between Leningrad and Moscow consisting of sleeping cars only.

I shall go to Leningrad and come back . . . how simple it is now! It's difficult to get used to it.

25th February, 1944. Leningrad

Here I am in Leningrad, and as yet there is no 'Arrow'. My typewriter is in Moscow; without it I'm like a person without hands. How many times have I told myself that I should not have been parted from it.

26th February, 1944

Apparently the 'Arrow' will leave, after all, on the 1st–2nd March, and I shall wait till that happens.

27th February, 1944

Yesterday I went to the Jubilee celebrations of the Botanical Institute; it is 230 years old.

The festivities took place in the grounds of the Botanical Gardens, in a small log house. Very well heated. It was delightful, when coming in from the hard frost outside, to see on the Presidium table lilies of the valley and white lilac, and to smell their scent.

Scientific and technical members of the Institute staff were sitting in the hall. There were many children. There was a particularly nice child in the second row. She looked like a lily of the valley, in a white bonnet and a little green fur coat.

We listened to a report on the work of the Institute, which before the war had maintained links with all the countries of the world. Plants from the Pamirs, Kashgar, Egypt, Brazil grow here; all this, naturally, besides the flora of the U.S.S.R. The Botanical Gardens sprang from the Apothecaries' Kitchen Garden, as long ago as the time of Peter the Great. The number of visitors is second only to those of the Moscow Museum of the Revolution. The Herbaria of Peter himself were lost in the fire of 1812. But the plants collected by the personal physician of the Empress Elizabeth are still preserved. We were shown thick pages of bluish paper, on each of which a plant was stuck with the greatest care, up to the thinnest tendril. Under each plant, inscriptions were written in Latin in an old-fashioned handwriting: 'Found near Poltava', 'Found in Holland, near the city of Leyden', 'Guinea Pepper'.

We have learned that plants—even those we think as dead—can live almost for ever. Traces of colouring have been found on cornflower petals and poppies in tombs of the Pharaohs.

The Herbaria have only two enemies—damp and careless treatment.

The main work of the Institute during the war—'vegetable growing and help to the Red Army'.

'Vegetable maps' were drawn up by the Institute.

Hips from the North and vitamins from pine needles were studied.

Medicinal balsams for hospitals were prepared and being manufactured.

The contents of vitamins in plant-tops was discovered.

Substitutes for manure were found.

Mushroom spawn and cigarette tobacco were cultivated.

Great work has been carried out in introducing and encouraging the use of 'wild plants' for food.

For the first time, the most valuable drug for heart disease, digitalis, was cultivated that far in the North—with Blockade conditions to make it more difficult.

Flowers were grown for hospitals, which in a way made up for the lack of food in some cases. They acted like vitamins of a sort, only through sight and sense of smell. Nikolai Ivanovich Kurnakov (the Botanist) once received an acknowledgement for some flowers from a convalescent soldier, and an assurance that he will 'hit the enemy even harder'.

During the Blockade the Botanical Gardens supplied the city with twenty million vegetable seedlings. One hundred and fifty special vegetable-growers were engaged on this work.

Workers of the Institute defended nine dissertations for the degree of doctor of biological sciences, and eight for the degree of candidate.

S. V. Sokolov ended his report with the words that 'Leningrad, freed from the enemy, must become even more beautiful than it was before the war' and 'that means it will need trees and flowers, and that valuable plants from all over the world must once again be gathered together under the glass roof of our Botanical Gardens'.

Later, there were speeches and greetings, in particular from a 'neighbour and relation'—the 'Institute of Vaccines and Serums'. Bacteria are also plants, only very minute.

We left after the distribution of Certificates of Honour by the Leningrad Soviet, and before the concert.

The cloakroom was full of children. The woman attendant declared:

'I shall only admit those who are accompanied by their mothers.'

A little girl answered proudly:

'My mother is already inside and has received a Certificate of Honour.'

29th February, 1944

Still no sign of the 'Arrow'. People say that the Oktyabrskaya line is not quite safe. The Germans are still attacking it and a great many mines are there. I don't know exactly why, but there is no 'Arrow'.

Evening

It has been decided that I'm to go to Moscow in an ordinary train.

12th March, 1944. Moscow

My affairs are progressing excellently, though they are entirely business affairs, there is absolutely no time to work. And I do so much want to settle down with the Diaries.

Just now—an announcement on the radio. The first inhabited locality in the Odessa region appeared in the news.

14th March, 1944

The story of a child who was being taken to Leningrad secretly by her parents. (Officially, this is still strictly prohibited.)

'I was put into a holder for rugs. The Control arrived, touched the holder, and I went all soft, like a pillow, and kept silent. So I wasn't found, after all.'

20th March, 1944. Leningrad

I went to Moscow in an ordinary train, but returned to Leningrad in the first 'Arrow' train.

Our international carriage was practically filled with writers, journalists and press photographers from all the Moscow papers. The train was festive and impressive. The driver was a hero of Socialist Labour, the men and women attendants

Leningraders who worked outstandingly during the Blockade.

From the carpet in the corridors, to the buttons on the attendants' blue jackets, everything was new and was spotlessly clean. The journey took twenty hours.

We could not tear ourselves away from the window until it got dark outside. In the morning we were glued to them again.

Bologoye, Lyubam, Tosno, all these 'Radishchev'* places were in ruins. Our train went slowly over temporary bridges, just put up. Everywhere there are still notices in Russian and German: 'Mines', 'Caution'. The former bridge over the river Tosno was particularly frightening. Blown-up supports and spans which collapsed from a great height into the water.

New telegraph poles look as white as candles, replacing old ones, burned or cut down by the Germans.

In other places our train trvaelled through a corridor of German dugouts and firing posts—they were that close to the railway. One of the permanent firing posts, destroyed by a direct hit, had spewed out its entire innards—concrete plates, pieces of corrugated iron, a machine-gun, remains of a sofa, a broken case of machine-gun belts. A rotting German overcoat and a pair of cramped hands show greenish from beneath the snow at the entrance.

What heroic labour was needed to reconstruct this line! It was specially daunting to look at Kolpino, at the shattered, half-burned, tortured Izhorsky works, painted with spots and zig-zags for camouflage.

We passed the Porcelain Factory, and there were we, under the roof of the Moscow Station in Leningrad, and the citizens of Leningrad came to meet us. All the time, during the journey, I was thinking of how I came to Leningrad from Moscow, to that vary station, nearly three years ago. A whole lifetime lay, gripped in a vice, between those two trains.

24th March, 1944

Quiet, tranquillity, absence of 'alerts' and shellings—all this has a strange effect on me. Evidently one doesn't get used to the feeling of security at once.

Work makes slow progress in this quiet. Only my bad health is active and varied. It would appear that the various ailments

* An eighteenth-century writer who wrote *The Journey from St. Petersburg to Moscow.*

that got worse during the Blockade, only now attack a person thoroughly. Interesting that I am not the only one to complain about this.

25th March, 1944

An article in the *Leningrad Pravda* about maps found on German gunners taken prisoner. The entire city was divided up not only into squares, but also into separate objectives, each under a corresponding number. Amongst 'objectives' that had to be destroyed—schools, museums, hospitals, the Hermitage, the Kirov Theatre,* our Medical Institute (Objective No. 89).

28th March, 1944

I went twice to the 'Public Health Exhibition'. The work began while we were still under the Blockade and being heavily shelled. And the organisers were much afraid that a shell would shatter all their exhibits to smithereens.

At the solemn opening, we the Presidium moved in a large group from the auditorium towards a number of exhibition rooms. The entry to them was barred by the traditional silk ribbon. The scissors were handed to the head of the Leningrad garrison, General Stepanov. I was standing next to him. He courteously passed the scissors to me, and I cut the ribbon.

An outstanding exhibit was a huge panorama of the Ladoga Route—'the route of life', without which Leningrad would hardly have survived.

Minute signals lit up, and manœuvring amongst bomb craters in a haze of snow and grey frost, the lorries move once again—but this time they are the size of match boxes. They are laden with food going in the direction of the city and going away from it with evacuees. And in the most dangerous spots, in the tensest situations, there was always the Red Cross, always a Leningrad doctor, nurse, public order volunteer or a girl orderly.

I remembered a wonderful thing—the emblem of Van Tulp, a Dutch doctor at the time of the Netherlands Revolution. It showed a half-burned candle in an antique candlestick (a high bright flame) and an inscription: 'In serving others, I burn'.

In a long, narrow room, there was a large diaorama showing the evacuation of wounded from units fighting on the Pulkovo

* Formerly the Imperial Maryinsky Opera House.

heights. Pulkovo again! The battle is in progress, and the wounded man either crawls along the trench himself, or is carried on a stretcher to the Battalion's first-aid post. From there, a dog pulls a kind of trough to the Regimental Medical Station, and from there the casualty is taken by horse in a cart to the Medical Centre. This has been set up, still in the line of fire, in the cellar of a half-destroyed house. And only from there does the casualty go by car to a Leningrad hospital.

It is intended that the exhibition should become a permanent museum, and this is very right. Here it is shown how the medical personnel worked in the days of the siege; how operations were performed near a wall that had on the street side of it a notice which said clearly: 'This wall is the most dangerous one during shelling'. Or, during hours when the sirens wailed, the A.A. guns roared, and one could hear the bombs thudding down, near ones at times. This is as it was in 1941, when Professor Dzhanelidze was operating, and I.D. and I were also present.

In the spectators' gallery students of both sexes and young doctors from neighbouring service hospitals sat on benches behind a barrier.

A girl was brought in with a smashed thigh, and anaesthetised. Dzhanelidze cut through the muscles and, overcoming the resistance of the bone ends to move apart, with a few movements slid a small scoop underneath the area in which the bone lay still, edge to edge, thus facilitating his task. Even an ignoramus like myself could appreciate and admire the strength and elegance of his work, the freedom and assurance of his hands. In the beginning, minute splinters of bone were extracted, and carelessly, as it seemed to me, thrown into a glass jar (in my simplicity, I thought they wouldn't be needed any more); they were put back in their proper place again.

What I did know about, and what did register, was the cleanliness and quietness—not a single spot on the floor, not a bloodstained plug. Even the steriliser lids, when dulled by steam, were wiped until they shone again. The operating theatre was put in order as the operation progressed. There was no sign of nerves, only occasionally did we hear the clink of metal against glass, or a short sentence spoken, a command or a directive.

Suddenly the sirens shattered this concentrated quiet. The

thunder of A.A. guns and the drone of planes grew louder and closer at a threatening rate. The ground swayed, glasses rattled. Those sitting on the benches turned involuntarily towards the exit.

'The operation is not yet finished,' Dzhanelidze said harshly, in his guttural voice.

And only when the raid got too close did they move the table to a room without windows.

10th April, 1944

The liberation of Odessa! There were two salutes today—one for the Army, and the other in honour of the Black Sea Fleet.

24th April, 1944

My health is disgusting, it wears me out. What if I take a good dose of my typewriter and write an essay for *Izvestiya* called 'The Time Has Come'?

THE TIME HAS COME

At the beginning of the winter, in one of the districts of the Kirovsky Prospekt, an approved type of a brick indoor stove was installed. These stoves were small, but gave out a good heat and were economical in fuel consumption. It was strange to see all these little bricks, dampers, doors and pipes lying out in the street in the winter snow. The Leningrad boys loved to squat, peeping into the stoves as if they could feel the warmth of a fire there. It was the fire of imagination.

Now it is spring. The birds are chirping in a lively way, and perching on the stove pipes. The spring sun is gently warming the experimental brick, rain washes it clean. It is possible that these stoves will soon be removed. But it seems to me they will stay in the memories of many of us as a real warmth symbolising a purely Leningrad quality—the organising and care by the city for the needs of its people.

Our street clocks have the same symbolic meaning.

One of the first things to suffer when the shelling and the bombing started were these clocks. Some of them collapsed in a heap of rubble with the falling wall, others, half torn off, swayed on their iron bases like weather vanes. Others again were full of their own glass splinters, and one look at them caused a sharp pain in the eyes. Others looked intact, but they had stopped.

The clocks showed different times in different parts of the town: half past two, five minutes to twelve, a quarter past five. That was the time when the blast or the weakening of the electric current or a fault in their mechanism hit them—it was the moment of their downfall.

There was a time when these street clocks were full of life. They regulated our lives—times of work, of rest, longed-for assignations, occupation, holidays and birthdays. In the evenings they shone from afar like ripe amber fruit with the pips showing black—those were the figures. All this has come to a standstill, died or gone numb with the beginning of the Blockade. Time has ceased to exist.

I can't forget how once, on a grim, freezing evening, when the siren was wailing, I looked up at one of the street clocks, and, instead of its dial, I saw the black circle of the night sky with hostile bright stars. This was in the dark days of 1942.

And now—in the spring of 1944—what a joy it is to see a ladder leaning against a street clock, and a man on the ladder! He repairs the clock carefully, painstakingly. And not at once, but tentatively, as if learning their work anew, the hands move from the spot. And move, move, move.... Time is coming back. It has come back!

After the street clocks, often at the same time, the window-panes too are gradually being restored.

Window glass is the most fragile, the most vulnerable, part of a building, the 'apple of its eye'. Window glass is not only the eye of a buidling, it is also part of the city's beauty.

We say 'the sun plays on the glass', and so it does. Without this 'play' of light, the buildings lose at once their vitality. Glass panes are receptive and impressionable, they blaze at sunset, turn blue during a thunderstorm and gleam silver in the moonlight.

The Gatchina glass factory Druzhnaya Gorka has started to work again after its destruction by the Germans. By the 1st of May it will give Leningrad its first consignment of window glass. And we, as we walk along the streets, rejoice at the sight of each new pane of glass, as a clear sign of the rebirth of the city.

However, the eyes are not the whole person, yet. Glass windows aren't all of the building. Here, as with human beings too, the frame is important. Houses, like people, are subject to a 'cosmetic' overhaul (it is actually called that way) as well as a capital one. For all renovations, building materials are necessary, and what matters most—people, people.

And the people of Leningrad are now repairing their town with the same energy they showed in defending it. Everything is being done without outside help, from the 'Great Earth'.* It's the same 'internal resources', from within themselves. Their reserve is inexhaustible.

Nowadays, we read the Leningrad newspapers as if they were bulletins on the health of a wounded but speedily recovering convalescent. Every day the arteries are better, every day his pulse is stronger.

After a long break, the soap factory has been re-started. The piano factory, Krasny Oktyabr, has produced its first twenty-five instruments during February and March—and most noteworthy is the fact that the first of these pianos will be sent to theatres in Novosibirsk and Belorussia. The city of Lenin not only supplies itself with everything it needs, it helps other towns as well.

The architectural department of the Art School is training specialist craftsmen in sculptural modelling and painting and decorating ceilings. Here, the history of styles and of architecture as well as descriptive geometry are being studied—in short everything necessary for restoring buildings of artistic value.

One of the victims of Fascist barbarity is the magnificent Senate Building, built by Rossi 110 years ago.

The roof and the inside of the building were damaged by bombing, but Themis, the Goddess of Justice, was untouched in her niche under the burnt-out dome, surrounded as she was by fallen statues of mutilated allegorical figures. During the most terrifying moments she held her scales without shaking, as if attesting thereby that the judgement of history on Hitler was yet to come. The Senate Building is going to be restored now, as well as the Kirov Theatre. Its stage was damaged by shells.

Benches are being painted in the gardens and parks of Leningrad, and fences repaired. Two thousand trees and twelve thousand shrubs will be planted. Soon the sun will shine again on tree trunks, in places where we used to see black

* Unoccupied territories of the Soviet Union.

gun barrels. Once again, birds will build their nests in places where machine-gun nests used to be.

Is there anyone who doesn't remember the minute allotment at the foot of Suvorov's monument, in front of the Kirov Bridge? Cabbage seedlings anxiously pressed themselves against the bronze pedestal of Mars. The God of War protected this modest piece of horticulture with his raised sword.

This was in the summer before last. Last summer, humble marigolds were in bloom round this monument. This year, who knows, we may see roses.

This is the history of wartime Leningrad, written, not on white leaves of paper, but on the green leaves of plants.

And the allotments themselves; for two years they took the place of all the lawns and flower-beds, and now they will spread even further, but this time, in many suburbs and dacha gardens so recently occupied by the enemy.

But for a long time to come the allotment gardener's spade will strike shell fragments or tangles of barbed wire. And the gardener, bending his head in reverence, will give some thought to the immortal earth of Leningrad, which endured all and conquered all.

29th April, 1944

I am settling down to work. It is the most reliable remedy, soothing all pain, and which never fails. Which never will fail....

The weather is rather grey and rainy . . . luckily.

3rd May, 1944

The Exhibitiion at our Writers' Union opens today. Also the Presidium, a banquet, etc. And I am *hors de combat* again. My début on the 1st of May cost me dear, particularly my climb to the tower on the roof of the anatomical department. It was from there that we looked down on the salute, and there that I was blown by all the winds of the Neva.

Am I really going to be immobile for the rest of my life? And it was I who dreamed of driving along the whole of the Pulkovo Meridian—not only on the globe.

6th May, 1944

Today it is winter again. I gave readings in the hospital and the Inzhenerny Zamok. I am gradually starting to walk.

8th May, 1944

In what does the so-called wisdom of life consist? In conquering circumstances when it is possible, to be clever enough to submit to circumstances when it's otherwise impossible. I shall give an example, as an explanation.

I counted on this spring being a joyful, active and triumphant one for me. But things happened otherwise. Instead—a serious illness which is apparently going to alter my life for a long time to come. No travelling at all—just staying at home.

Yesterday I went to town and came back literally half alive.

Our radio has started to work at last, though still not very well. And yesterday, too, after a long break, the announcement of our success at Sebastopol.

9th May, 1944

We have liberated Sebastopol. The whole of the Crimea is clear of Germans.

13th May, 1944

Yesterday I went to speak at the Baltic works. As a farewell gesture, Leningrad has revealed itself to me in all the charm of its White Nights, just beginning, and, before that, in the brilliance of the sunset.

As we crossed the Neva and the canals, the water kept changing colour, becoming ever more beautiful.

At the Baltic works, in the gaps between the cranes and the iron girders, the sky was the colour of doves' wings.

Nevertheless, farewell Leningrad! Our life together is nearing its end.

14th May, 1944

Put our belongings in order—packing away our warm things for the summer. As always, the orderliness soothed me, but I had a distressing night.

As often happens, spring has come all of a sudden. Yesterday we went to town. Doors and windows were wide open in the warm streets, the city was covered with a haze like hot breath. Already dust was swirling, already there was insufficient oxygen for leaves that hadn't fully opened. And I, dragging myself along on leaden feet, felt very depressed. . . . Can it really be that I am doomed to the life of immobility? What about all the travelling I haven't yet achieved?

19th May, 1944

Conducted a discussion at the Writers' Union for novice writers, on the subject 'What is Inspiration?'

21st May, 1944

Spoke indifferently at the Primorsky District Committee. I was very tired. And at the end I would like so much to do everything very well.

25th May, 1944

Took leave of the Botanical Gardens. We spent a long time in Greenhouse No. 22—'Noah's Ark', as members of the staff call it. Here, plants of three adjacent climates live as neighbours: palms, ferns, cacti, orchids, rice ears and begonias. All the plants are quite young and were cultivated during the time of the Blockade. The Blockade banana trees are so tall that they are already pushing against the glass roof of the hot-house. The temperature in the 'arc' is as it should be—16–18 degrees. The thermometer hangs nearby.

A fantastic plant is growing in a transparent aquarium. It comes from Madagascar, and is called Uvirandra Fenestralis, which means living in a window.

Even in such a paradise of warmth as Madagascar, Uvirandra is evidently looked on as an indoor plant, and it is easy to believe this by looking at its leaves. They may be the most delicate of all the flora in creation, consisting only of rather dark veins, without a trace of the usual green cellulose. It is the lightest vegetable canvas, studded with air bubbles.

Uvirandra lacks tadpoles. When they are let loose in the aquarium, they take off and swallow the thin air bubbles, and clean the leaves, making them look just like satin. But the tadpoles disappeared as long ago as the Finnish campaign, when all the tiny rivers and swamps were mined.

The young cacti stand in rows on the shelves. They were the favourite children of Nikolai Ivanovich Kurnakov, who died recently. During the first winter of the Blockade, Kurnakov saved the cacti by taking them home and keeping them warm by his little stove. His wife used to clean them with a small brush, finding her way carefully between the prickles. A cactus falls to pieces and dies as soon as its pores get clogged.

We saw the bust of Engels, on a tall pedestal, at the entrance to the log house known to us from last year's exhibition and celebrations in honour of the 230th anniversary of the Gardens. One of the first editions of the *Dialectic of Nature* was beside him in a glass case.

Last year the entire exhibition was dedicated to 'wild' plants, those modest vitamin carriers. We came on this list of dishes in a brochure issued at that time: 'Zrazy with Burdock', 'Roulet with Goose Foot', 'Ragout from Kupyr', 'Caviar from Dandelions'—it would provoke a smile if it weren't so tragic.

Now the wild plants are only a supporting element to real edible roots grown in allotments.

In the next room, as well as the specially cultivated medicinal plants, such as belladonna, balderian, altea, foxglove—wild plants are also hung on the walls:—lily of the valley, henbane, camomile, lime, wormwood, buckthorn. Many of them are toxic and beneficial at the same time (dialectic of nature).

I saw here a Zikuta in formalin, and also heard for the first time that it wasn't the cause of Socrates' death, as is commonly thought, but that it was another poisonous plant—hemlock. Be that as it may, the sight of Zikuta still fills me with fear. It is a thick round root stock with poisonous glands, like those of a snake. They oxydise in the air and turn orange. String-like roots come off the main rootstock.

In the spring of 1942, when starving people hurled themselves at every root, at every little leaf, it was most important for them to recognise poisonous plants.

The round greenhouse, No. 28, where the Victoria Regina grew in a pond, was damaged three times. Once by a bomb, and twice by direct hits from shells. It has been smashed again, after we saw it last year.

The Victoria Regina, born in the warm lagoons of the Amazon, is a puzzle. Up till now it is not known exactly whether it is an annual, in its homeland, or only here, with us, where it can't get enough light and heat. The German bombs and shells have 'decided' this question in their own way—they have killed the plant and damaged the hot-house.

We left the exhibition and were already walking down an avenue when from behind someone shouted:

'Don't sit on those brightly coloured benches, they have just been painted!'

The refurbirshing of the Gardens has already begun.

27th May, 1944

We have taken our leave of Dr. Messel. This is probably our last visit to his domain, the Central Station of first-aid service which worked through the most difficult days like a good clock—efficiently and without stopping.

I glanced through their log books. The day of 19th September, 1941, when we went to Razyezhaya is fully written up. Then two first-aid nurses on duty were injured, 'Alekseeva Zinaida—injury to the thorax and both shin bones; Markova Valentina—injury to the right eye'.

During this raid four heavy high-explosive bombs were dropped on the Dmitriyevsky Pereulok, only 245 metres long.

Yes indeed, all this happened. We lived through all this.

29th May, 1944

Now I have finally learned everything about digitalis on the cultivation of which Monteverdi was engaged.

In its wild state digitalis grows only in the Harz Mountains and in Thuringia. In order not to spend foreign currency on importing it, we started to cultivate it in the Northern Caucasus and in Belorussia, but all this was stopped by the war.

The trouble with digitalis is that it doesn't keep for long in storage. By the spring of 1942 old digitalis stocks in Leningrad had completely lost their curative powers, and the city Health Administration gave orders to withdraw them from the network of the Health Service.

Therefore, what had to be done next? The heart muscle never knows complete rest, it had to go through particularly testing times during the Blockade, and it needed drugs. So a proposal was submitted to the Botanical Institute by the Leningrad Soviet to grow their own foxgloves, and to prepare the drug by the autumn.

Monteverdi himself, who was in charge of the curative plants, was at the time in our hospital with severe distrophy, a patient of Professor Tushinsky.

As soon as he was a little better, he started to work.

In the 'archives' of the Gardens a small quantity of the

necessary seeds was discovered, but the germinating potential was unknown. And the most vital thing—there was no time to grow a perennial plant (it was thought that only the perennial's qualities were beneficial). They had to make an annual fox-glove work as a perennial. At first the seeds were planted in a greenhouse, later in a hot-house, later still in the ground. A struggle began for a growing 'area': there was little suitable ground and foxglove leaves reach sixty centimetres in diameter.

In order to speed up the harvesting, and to economise on space, Monteverdi and his helpers made an innovation: consecutive gathering of the leaves as they ripen. The outside leaves were taken off first, so that the inner ones developed more rapidly.

The leaves were very succulent, whereas dry ones were needed. So they dried them in an empty derelict house, by hanging them on ropes, like washing. Only later did the Pharmaceutical Institute provide special driers which were heated by the remains of the house, which was finally broken up for this purpose.

At last, by the autumn, as it had been proposed, the digitalis was ready. The efficiency of the drug had to be checked. How-ever, on whom? It is usually tested on frogs, but if tadpoles had disappeared, grown-up frogs were even harder to find. So the doctors decided to try the drug out on themselves. It turned out to be so effective that it was necessary to reduce the usual dosage.

Not only did Leningrad get the precious remedy, it was even exported behind the 'Ring', to the Great Earth.

When Monteverdi concluded his story I asked whether he had had the chance to try the drug on himself. He brightened up as he answered that yes, digitalis had 'helped' him very much, because as soon as the City Committee proposed that he, Monteverdi, should do this experiment, he felt a great upsurge of energy, and left the clinic before he was supposed to do so.

Shipchinsky told me that the administration of the Botanical Gardens is far more complicated than that of the Zoo. Animals can express their needs vocally, while plants are silent. They die if people don't guess what their needs are. It is curious that horticulturists completely lose their sense of smell on account of humid air. They are no more aware of the scent of flowers than deaf Beethoven was of hearing his music.

Before the war, two thousand tons of coal were used each year for heating the greenhouses. During the Blockade, nine-tenths of all the plants perished from cold. The only ones saved were in small greenhouses or in the homes of officials, as, for instance, the cacti at Kurnakov's. The most hardy turned out to be the rhododendrons with their thick, fleshy leaves.

When I learned that the damage caused to the Gardens by the war was calculated at 1,200,000 gold roubles, I asked, how did one reach this figure? Was it possible that each tree was taken into account? And what about the labour spent on it?

It turns out that everything is counted in quite a different way. One million two hundred thousand gold roubles represent the cost of five journeys around the world, which will be necessary to restore the Gardens to their pre-war state.

The journeys must be to:

1. The tropics of South America.
2. West Africa (Belgian Congo).
3. Indian Ocean: Madagascar, Ceylon (Colombo), India, Singapore, Buitenzorg Botanical Gardens in Java.
4. Eastern Australia—as well as New Zealand and Tasmania.
5. South-east China.

All these are basic growing centres, the cradles of plants. Our own country, though vast, is so mainly in longitude and for botany latitude is necessary.

Transplanting mature trees to different climates isn't easy. Trees are moved from their native ground into buckets where they spend two years getting used to different soils. And only then can they be despatched to another distant country.

Monteverdi and Shipchinsky left. As a parting present, they gave me three little ferns and a begonia. I went on thinking about the Botanical Gardens for a long time. It went through my entire life in Leningrad like a 'green thread'.* The Gardens met me in August 1941, and saw me off in May 1944. The Pulkovo Meridian, crossing Leningrad at a few points, passes along the lawns of the Gardens as well.

I looked at my poor little globe, at all those seas and continents, flowing with blood now, and I thought about the

* It is a paraphrase of the common Russian expression, to 'pass like a red thread' through a literary work, speech or suchlike, used long before the revolution.

time when the war will be over and those five journeys around the world became possible. 'Buitenzorg Botanical Gardens on Java . . .' The name alone!

The round earth all in gardens rose in front of me ('Plants unfurling the incalculable surface of their leaves . . .'). And on this earth—bright peaceful generations, for the happiness of which my country has done so much. And in particular— Leningrad.

5th June, 1944

My farewell evening at the Writers' Union was fine and warm, like today's weather.

6th June, 1944

Though I still find it difficult to move, I nevertheless decided this morning to visit the exhibition, 'The Defence of Leningrad'. I couldn't go away to Moscow without seeing it.

I.D. and I went by tram to the Lebyazhaya Kanavka, and from there we went slowly along the sunny side up to the Solyanoy Gorodok, where the exhibition is being held. It was a lovely day, the first really warm one. It was hard to tear oneself away from the greenery, warmed by the sunshine, and enter the huge cold building. At the entrance, on every captured enemy gun, sat one live Leningrad boy.

The exhibition is very large. I couldn't see all of it. We didn't visit the basement part at all, but we had a thorough look at the main halls.

I.D. and I talked very little—a nod of the head, a gesture, a word, and we understood each other. Nearly three years of our lives passed before us.

Here had been collected everything that had threatened Leningrad, and everything that saved it.

German helmets were piled up against a wall in the main hall in a triangular heap which reached nearly to the ceiling. In the centre—heavy German guns for shelling military objectives, among them our hospital, objective No. 89; 154 mm guns with barrels as wide as the fire-box of a railway engine, six barrel flame-throwers. 'Panthers', 'Tigers', 'Ferdinands', painted in green or the colour of granite, or snow white. A shot-down plane with a black cross on the wings, shells and bombs of all types. A magnetic naval mine dropped near the Baltic railway station by the Germans, but which luckily failed to explode.

We met 'our' bomb here as well, the one that was dropped on our grounds on a golden autumn day in 1941. Under the bomb an inscription: 'Weight 1000 kilogrammes, diameter 660 mm, length 990 mm. On the 1st of October, 1941, defused by Engineer Captains N. G. Lopatin and Commander of the Home Guard A. P. Ilyinsky.'

The bomb was intact except for a piece of the stabiliser which is lying in my table drawer at home.

A decorative panel—the first in the history of aerostatics, aerial ramming by the young pilot, Savostiyanov, on the night of 5th October. He brought down an enemy plane and then descended by parachute. A gigantic gun from the battleship *Oktyabrskaya Revoluziya* took up the entire length of another hall, and, near it, raised above the floor, as if it were skimming over the waves, a torpedo launch badly holed, whose crew had performed miracles of bravery.

19th September, 1941 (the day we arrived in Razyeszhaya Street a few minutes after the bomb fell), turned out to be one of the bloodiest days of the Blockade. There were six alerts, lasting a total of seven hours thirty-four minutes.

528 high explosives were dropped

1435 incendiary bombs

97 artillery shells were fired at the city.

89 hits were registered.

Three thousand nine hundred and twelve batteries of the town anti-aircraft defence centre, 52 crews of local A.A. defence centres, 17 voluntary ambulance squads of the All Union Red Cross Organisation, and 21 self groups of residential dwellings were at work.

The Section on Leningrad Industry. This devoted itself and its work to the Front to the exclusion of everything else. Turbine generators from local works have been sent to Komsomolsk, Rubzovsk, Baku, Briansk, Stalingrad, to the Donetz Basin—Makeevka, Gorlovka, Kadiyevka, by the time the Blockade ended.

The tobacco factory which manufactured 'Festival', 'Zephyr', 'Northern Palmyra' cigarettes before the war, the scent factory and the factory making yoghurt worked during the Blockade for defence. And now, once again, we see the scent 'White Night' in shop windows. True, the carton is slightly less elegant, but the little yoghurt bottles, which appeared again, contain soya instead of milk.

The Public Nutrition Section. Food and menus of Leningrad's canteens during the Blockade.

Root flour, sweepings (that is all the remains swept from everywhere), were used for scones.

Albumen yeast—for first dishes.

Dextrine (technical waste)—for fritters, baked puddings, rissole cutlets.

Flour from linseed cakes—for second dishes.

Cellulose—for fritters, baked puddings, rissole cutlets.

Belt (part of a textile machine made of pigskin, which couldn't be used any longer)—for soup, meat jelly, cutlets.

Fish glue and the flesh side of hide—also for jellies.

On one of the shelves—'lighting utensils': a splinter, a lantern—paraffin lamp, called 'the flying bat', earthenware saucers (for oil wicks), test tubes, jars, candles.

Here I.D. and I looked at each other remembering those tortuous efforts to light hollow-bodied candles of unknown composition with wicks that never went through the middle, but emerged at the side hissing and fading away.

We spent a particularly long time, very long indeed, in front of a stand arranged as a bakery. The window was thickly covered with ice, only the centre was partly melted by the meagre warmth of two oil wicks.

And in this clear space, a pair of scales; four small weights on one side—on the other, 125 grammes of bread, the amount the majority of the citizens of Leningrad received from the 20th November to the 25th December, 1941.

Above the scales in a glass retort was the flour of that time, and a note of its composition:

Flour, rye defective—50%
Salt—10%
Cake—10%
Cellulose—15%
Soya flour, hack dust, bran, each—5%

After the exhibition I.D. went to town on business, and I stayed to sit for a while on a bench in the Summer Garden.

The garden was beautiful, fragrant and full of fresh greenery. Children were running up and down the avenues, wearing wreaths of dandelions. The Krylov monument was dappled with sunlight. Its timber protection is about to be removed.

Sun—warmth—quiet, hardly audible rustle of leaves. . . . I sat, spellbound.

A woman came and sat next to me. Pale, yellowish skin, shortness of breath. It was still the Blockade pallor. I remembered: 50% flour, rye defective. . . .

When the woman regained her breath she said she was feeling much better now, that she is already walking without help, and is it true that a 'Second Front has been opened?' She had just heard about it in the town.

I didn't know anything. I had left home early in the morning and the radio wasn't working.

I hurried home. And there I learned that it was true. The Allies have landed in Northern France.

7th June, 1944

It seems we are going to Moscow on Monday, the 12th.

Farewell Leningrad! Nothing in the world will ever erase you from the memory of those who lived here through this time.